By the same author

Suzanne's
Cooking
Secrets

Suzanne Warner Pierot

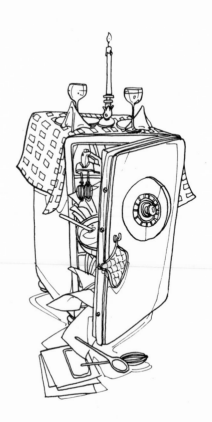

SUZANNE'S COOKING SECRETS

Illustrated by Anthony Kramer

W · W · NORTON & COMPANY

NEW YORK   LONDON

Copyright © 1981 by Suzanne Warner Pierot
Published simultaneously in Canada by George J. McLeod Limited, Toronto.
Printed in the United States of America
All Rights Reserved
First Edition

Designed by Earl Tidwell

Library of Congress Cataloging in Publication Data

Pierot, Suzanne.
  Suzanne's cooking secrets.

  Includes index.
  1. Cookery. I. Title. II. Title: Cooking secrets.
TX652.P529 1981   641.5   80–39492
ISBN 0–393–01458–4
ISBN 0–393–00055–9 (pbk.)

W. W. Norton & Company, Inc. 500 Fifth Avenue, New York, N.Y. 10110
W. W. Norton & Company Ltd. 25 New Street Square, London EC4A 3NT

1 2 3 4 5 6 7 8 9 0

For the men in my life,

Jacques, Michael,
Chris, Jeff, Teddy,
Henry Victor, Henri Maurice, Jack

food lovers all

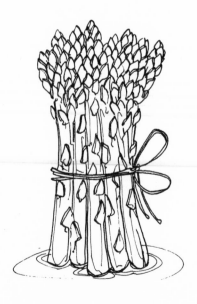

Contents

Introduction

This book has been written by a squirrel. Me. A tidy squirrel, but a squirrel nevertheless. One of those persons who clips interesting newspaper articles, makes a note of the tag line of a joke, and carefully files the names of restaurants around the world should, perchance, I ever find myself in that country.

I don't know if I'm bragging or confessing when I say that I can easily find all this material at a moment's notice. I think confessing is probably nearer the mark because all that filing makes me sound so darn methodical, which I don't think I really am. Although I do believe that the three essentials for every bride are a stove, filing cabinet, and a bed, not necessarily in that order. Even a one-drawer cabinet makes it possible to have folders for such dissimilar ideas as "Places I Would Like to Visit," "Clever Decorating Ideas," "Children's Report Cards" as well as "Bills," "Receipts," and "Cancelled Checks." A filing cabinet makes it all so easy.

That's how I happened to have the material for this book—it's part of the file marked "Kitchen Ideas." All my life I've been making notes of any quick or novel way to do something in the kitchen. In fact as I go through my kitchen folder it's like looking at the T.V. show "This Is Your Life."

My mother was the home-economics editor of the *San Francisco Chronicle* and later, after I was born, she was the host of two of the first women's talk shows on radio, in both Los Angeles and San Francisco. In my teens I worked with her on those programs and learned tricks like "How to Match Cake Layers" (p. 126). It's such a simple idea, but once it has been pointed out to you, you wonder why you always had put up with lopsided cake layers that didn't fit back together properly when split. I learned so much from my mother—more than I knew at the time, but I guess all of us do and don't realize it until years later.

I figured out "How to Serve Hollandaise without Having to Make It at the Last Minute" (p. 42) when I lived in England and was in charge of Howard Hughes's film interests. I was very young and trying hard to seem older, as I thought befitted my job. Gracious no-fuss dinners at home for two or four were part of my self-image. You know the kind—where one course arrives after another with no apparent effort. No effort—ha! Well that's where the thermos trick with the Hollandaise fitted into my life story.

Later when my son Michael was going to school at the Lycée Français in London, I gave him oranges with the rind cut, as described in "Make an Orange 'Appeeling' to Kids" (p. 102). The orange was easier to peel and Mama's little darling would eat it rather than trade it for candy.

I was one of the founders of commercial television in London and our network was Associated TeleVision. By this time I was beyond the "casual" sumptuous dinner party stage and interested in Chinese cooking. One of my friends had a Chinese cook who taught me the trick of partially freezing meat and chicken in order to make paper-thin slices (p. 52).

Back in America my daughter Elena was born and I became part of the PTA. One of my Women's Club friends showed me the quick way to frost homemade cupcakes for 1 or 10 or 100 when you're the class mother (p. 130). The barbecue trick of dousing flames with lettuce leaves or a whisk broom (p. 154) belonged to this new domesticity. And so did cutting a pie in five pieces. Five *even* pieces (p. 127–8)!

And then one day my world stopped. I became a widow. Baking cupcakes and cutting pies into equal pieces no longer seemed such fun. Like all widows I had two choices to make after I had learned to live with some of the numbing hurt and sense of loss. I could either stay at home and mope or go out and do something with my life. I went back to work.

My work took me all over the world. I even found a use for my list of unusual restaurants in such diverse places as Taipei and Calcutta. A German woman taught me the paper-towel trick for fluffy rice (p. 138) and a new housekeeper revealed the secret of making instant coffee taste more like fresh brewed (p. 155).

And in my round-the-world whirl I met Jacques. Jacques Pierot III. Dutch by birth, French (Huguenot) by name, British by accent, and American (by naturalization). No one can tell me Fate or God doesn't have a hand in these things or how else would I have met this elegant, distinguished man. All this and a gourmet as well. So I was back to "Warming Plates for a Crowd" (p. 157).

I was also back to gardening with a vengeance, forgetting I had once told myself that "a garden is a thing of beauty and a *job* forever." I wrote *The Ivy Book: The Growing and Care of Ivy and Ivy Topiary, What Can I Grow in the Shade?*, and *Suzanne's Garden Secrets*, founded the American Ivy Society, and began lecturing on plants at the New York Botanical Gardens.

I reentered the world of home economics that I had learned about when I was on the radio talk show with my mother, threw myself into dinner parties, and acquired along the way a professional Garland stove.

"How to Make Half an Egg" (p. 27) became important as I halved soufflé recipes remembering Thomas Wolfe's words, "There is no spectacle on earth more appealing than that of a beautiful woman in the act of cooking dinner for someone she loves." A p.s. to that famous quote is found on p. 82–3, "Nobody Loves a Hand That Smells of Onion."

Meantime, as one of the founders of La Société des Gastronomes, I couldn't admit to one of my culinary fears. "If You Are Chicken When It Comes to Lobster" (p. 73) was one of the private secrets I never admitted.

As a member of the food committee of the International Wine and Food Society, a board member of Les Dames d'Escoffier, and as a Dame de la Chaîne of the Chaîne des Rôtisseurs, food-decorating secrets like "A Lemon That Will Never Be a 'Lemon' " (p. 103) and "Frosted Grapes" (p. 105) began to find their way into my filing cabinet.

So there you have it, the story of my life, and I only meant to tell you how I acquired my cooking secrets.

I owe great thanks to so many people who have helped me along the way with this book. Principally to Sylvia Dowling and Irena Chalmers, but mainly, as always, to Jacques.

Of course one of the great things about having a secret is to be able to share it with someone else. I hope you will use my collection of cooking secrets, add to them, and pass them along to your family and friends.

SUZANNE WARNER PIEROT

New York, 1981

Suzanne's
Cooking
Secrets

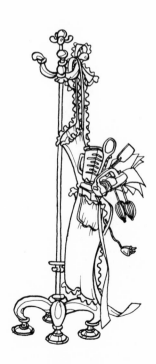

CHAPTER ONE

Eggs . . .
    Cheese . . .
        Appetizers

UNSTICKING A STUCK EGG

When an egg is stuck to its cardboard carton, don't try to pry it out. It usually breaks. Wet the carton and the egg will slip out more easily.

FIRST AID FOR A CRACKED EGG

If the shell cracks when you are boiling an egg, add a teaspoon of salt or vinegar to the water. This will prevent the egg white from escaping.

HOW TO BOIL A CRACKED EGG

Wrap the egg tightly in aluminum foil so the water will not get in and the egg will not get out.

A NEAT WAY TO PICK UP A BROKEN EGG

This trick is almost magical. If you drop an egg on the floor, pour some salt over the mess. Let it stand for a few minutes and then sweep it up.

BROWN VERSUS WHITE EGGS

No matter how you or I feel about brown versus white eggs, there is absolutely no nutritional difference or taste difference between the two. But when it comes to boiling them, there is indeed a difference. Brown shells are thicker than white and do not crack as easily when they are boiled.

TEST FOR EGG FRESHNESS

You don't have to be a chicken to know if you have a fresh egg before you boil it. To test for freshness, put the egg in a bowl of cold water. If it sinks, it is fresh. If it is fairly fresh, it will bob up on one end. If it is stale, it will float.

DIFFERENCE IN VOLUME BETWEEN EGG SIZES

If you want to know how much egg you get from the many different sizes of eggs, here is the answer. One cup of eggs is the equivalent of four extra large, five large, six medium or seven small eggs.

YOLKS IN THE WHITES

When you are separating eggs, if a speck of egg yolk falls into the egg whites, lift it out with an empty egg-shell half. Do not try to fish it out with your fingers; the oil on your skin will prevent the egg whites from expanding.

REMOVING THE SHELL FROM RAW EGGS

When breaking eggs, if you drop a piece of shell into the bowl, fish it out with a larger piece of egg shell. The two pieces of shell will cling together.

SAVING ENERGY

Even when you are hard boiling eggs, you can conserve energy. Boil the eggs for only three minutes. Then turn off the heat and let the eggs stand in the hot water for at least fifteen minutes. This is a good way of ensuring that the eggs are not overcooked. When eggs are cooked for too long the yolk turns a darker color.

REMOVING THE SHELL FROM HARD-BOILED EGGS

Once the egg is hard-boiled, put it immediately into a bowl of cold water. Remove the shell while the egg is still warm and you will not tear the egg white.

ANOTHER WAY TO SHELL EGGS I

If you want a hard-boiled egg to peel more easily, roll the egg under your hand on the counter, completely cracking the shell. The tough inner membrane will be loosened and the shell will slip off more easily.

ANOTHER WAY TO SHELL EGGS II

An easy way to remove the shell from hard-boiled eggs is to peel them under cold running water.

YET ANOTHER WAY OF SHELLING EGGS

Begin to peel the eggs from the large end to release the air pocket and the shells will slip off quickly.

CENTERING THE YOLK

When making stuffed or deviled eggs, turn the egg in the water several times while it is cooking and the yolk will stay in the center.

REMOVING THE YOLKS FROM HARD-BOILED EGGS

Cut the eggs in half using a sharp knife that has been dipped in cold water. Use your thumb to lift out the egg yolk.

ARRANGING STUFFED EGGS

To prevent stuffed eggs from sliding on the serving plate, use a touch of the filling to anchor the egg to the plate.

COOL SECRET FOR SLICING EGGS

Slice eggs after they have been chilled. They do not slice neatly if they are still warm or at room temperature. It also helps to wet the knife before each cut.

HOW TO STORE HARD-BOILED EGGS

To prevent the egg whites from becoming stiff and tough, remove the shell from the eggs while they are still warm and store the eggs in a jar filled with cold water.

HOW TO TELL IF THE EGG IS RAW

Did you ever find a couple of eggs on the refrigerator shelf and not remember whether they were hard-boiled or raw? Here's how to tell the difference without breaking the shell. The hard-boiled egg can be spun like a top. The uncooked egg will not spin.

HOW TO POACH EGGS AHEAD OF TIME

To poach eggs for a crowd for Sunday brunch, cook the eggs ahead of time, slighly undercooking them. Then slide them into a big bowl of cold water. When they are ready to be served, reheat in simmering water.

If you are making the eggs only a short while ahead, slide all of them—as they are cooked—into a big bowl of hot but not boiling water. Don't worry about them sticking together. Top with more hot water from time to time to keep them warm. The eggs will be soft, warm, and ready to eat when you are ready to serve them.

PERFECT BAKED EGGS

The secret is, of all things, brown paper. Put a piece of brown paper on top of the ramekin. The yolk will cook quickly and the white will not toughen.

FLUFFIER OMELETS

The secret to making a fluffier omelet is not to beat it. Just a few whooshes with your fork to blend the white and yolk is all you need to make a light, fluffy omelet. Overbeating makes the omelet tough. Hard to believe but true. And if you add one-half teaspoon of baking powder for every four eggs, you will get an even lighter omelet.

SHINY OMELETS

To make your completed omelet shine, brush it with a teaspoon of melted butter.

BEATING EGG WHITES I

Never attempt to beat egg whites in a plastic bowl. Plastic retains traces of grease no matter how clean it looks and feels. Adding a pinch of baking soda may help minimally, but it is better to use a copper, metal, glass, or ceramic bowl.

BEATING EGG WHITES II

Although this method is tiring, egg whites beaten in a copper bowl with a large balloon wire whisk increase to seven times their original volume because of the contact with the copper. Wipe the inside of the beating bowl with a paper towel dipped in white vinegar before you start beating.

If you are using a hand-held electric beater, add a little salt and one-eighth teaspoon cream of tartar to stabilize the whites. Hold the beater at a 45-degree angle and you will get an unusual volume of egg whites.

BEATING EGG WHITES III

I don't know why, but egg whites from eggs that have been refrigerated for a week or two produce a better and higher volume than fresh ones.

BEATING EGG WHITES IV

Egg whites at room temperature beat up to a greater volume. Break the eggs while cold and let them stand until they come to room temperature.

THE INSTANT EGG WARMER

When you do not have time to bring your eggs to room temperature, just put them gently into a bowl of warm water for a few minutes before breaking.

SEPARATING EGGS

The fresher the egg, the easier it is to separate. If you are not deft at separating eggs, break them, one at a time, into a cup. Hold a saucer over the cup and let the white pour out.

You will find it much easier to separate the yolk from the white of an egg if you do it as soon as it comes out of the refrigerator. A cold egg yolk is less likely to break than one at room temperature.

TOO MANY EGG YOLKS

To store unbroken egg yolks for up to four days, cover them with cold water and keep them in the refrigerator. Clean pimiento jars are good for storing two or three egg yolks.

MERINGUE TRICKS I

Egg whites for meringues should not be beaten so stiffly that they could be cut with a knife; beat only to the point where they hold a peak. They should be firm enough so that if you put a whole egg into the bowl of beaten egg whites, the whole egg stays on top and does not sink to the bottom of the bowl.

MERINGUE TRICKS II

If beaten egg whites are not used immediately they will become watery and the air that has been beaten into them will escape. Beat egg whites only when you are ready to use them. You can, however, hold them for up to fifteen minutes if you cover them with another bowl. Whites must be covered to prevent deflation yet need a little space for air circulation. Plastic wrap is too tight—an inverted bowl is just right.

SECRET TO ADDING SUGAR TO EGG WHITES

When you are beating egg whites and the recipe calls for sugar, add the sugar at the very end when the whites have formed soft peaks. If you put the sugar in at the beginning, the egg whites won't be as thick no matter how hard or long you beat. As a general rule, add one-quarter cup of sugar for each egg white.

TOO MANY EGG WHITES

Freeze extra egg whites in an ice-cube tray. After they are frozen store them in a plastic bag in the freezer. They thaw quickly.

EGG YOLKS CAN THICKEN SAUCE

If the sauce you are preparing is too thin, you can thicken it with a mixture of milk or cream and egg yolks. Use one tablespoon of cold milk or cream for each egg yolk. Two or three egg yolks with cream will thicken one cup of liquid. Slowly add two or three tablespoons of the prepared hot sauce to the yolk-cream mixture. When blended, return the mixture to the remaining hot sauce in the saucepan. Stir over low heat until hot but do not let the sauce boil or the egg yolks will scramble.

HOW TO KEEP THE WINE SOBER

When you're using wine in dishes that contain cream, butter, or eggs, add the wine first and the other ingredients won't curdle.

HOW TO MAKE HALF AN EGG

Beat the egg yolk and egg white together and use only half the quantity. Store the remaining half in a small jar with a tightly fitting lid such as an empty jar that held chopped pimientos. This is very useful when halving recipes that call for one egg.

HANDLING UNCOOKED SOUFFLÉ

Spoon the soufflé mixture gently into the soufflé dish. Do not let the mixture drop into the dish from a height or all the air will be expelled. The more air there is in the mixture, the more the soufflé will rise.

HOW TO GET A "HIGH HAT" ON A SOUFFLÉ

When making a soufflé give it that professional high-hat look by running your thumb around the inside of the dish, below the rim, before the soufflé is cooked. Put the soufflé in the oven and a "high hat" will rise in the center.

TAKING THE WIGGLE OUT OF MOZZARELLA

It is difficult to cut mozzarella cheese neatly unless you dip your knife in hot water before making each slice.

HOW TO KEEP CHEESE FRESH I

Whenever possible, serve only the quantity of cheese that you think will be eaten. If cheese is left at room temperature for too long it "sweats" butterfat and deteriorates rapidly.

HOW TO KEEP CHEESE FRESH II

Always rewrap cut cheese in fresh transparent wrap to keep out air. Wrap blue cheeses in cheesecloth drizzled with vinegar or port wine to extend their life. Overwrap them in aluminum foil. Store Parmesan and other hard cheeses in the vegetable drawer of the refrigerator. The humidity will prevent them from drying out.

GREAT GRATING IDEA I

Before grating cheese, put it in the freezer for about forty minutes. It won't be as sticky and will grate much more easily.

GREAT GRATING IDEA II

Rub the grater with a little vegetable oil to prevent cheese, orange, and lemon rind, and other ingredients from sticking to it.

HOW TO PREVENT BOXED CHEESE
FROM SINKING IN THE MIDDLE

Turn Brie, Camembert, Pont l'Évêque, and other boxed cheeses onto the reverse side every day or they will sink in the center.

DON'T SAY "CHEESE," SAVE IT

Don't throw away leftover cheese after a party. Save even the tiniest wedge, grate it, and freeze it in an airtight plastic bag. Add additional scraps as you have them. The grated frozen cheese melts in an instant and is great for chicken divan, veal parmigiana, omelets, soufflés, etc.

FREEZING AND THAWING CHEESE

Hard cheeses can be frozen very successfully. First wrap the cheese tightly in plastic wrap to exclude the air, then wrap in aluminum foil. When needed, thaw the cheese in the refrigerator. Do not remove the wrappings until the cheese has completely defrosted.

PREVENT CHEESE FROM BECOMING STRINGY

When making cheese sauce, add the cheese at the last moment and cook it slowly. If the sauce gets too hot, the cheese will become stringy. If this should happen, add one or two tablespoons of cold white wine and the sauce will become smooth again.

TIMESAVING WAY TO MAKE SANDWICHES

You will be a sandwich speed queen if you freeze the bread first. Food will spread more easily and the bread is less likely to tear.

KEEPING SANDWICHES FRESH

To keep sandwiches fresh and moist, cover them with damp paper towels or a kitchen towel that has been wrung out in cold water.

HOW TO LIMIT THE DRINKS

The saltier the hors d'oeuvres, the more thirsty will be the guests. So go easy on potato chips, pretzels, and salted nuts. These are served in cocktail bars so you will buy more drinks.

FASTEST WAY TO PREPARE CANAPÉS

If you are preparing dozens of canapés, the fastest way of handling the situation is to establish a conveyor-belt system. Do all of the buttering, then all of the whatever comes next. If you are working in a kitchen with the dimensions of a closet, spread out to another room or erect a series of surfaces.

FAST NO-COOK CANAPÉS I

For a low calorie, unusual canape, cut peeled cucumbers into one-half-inch rounds to use as a base instead of crackers. Spread with a little mayonnaise that has been flavored with a dash of curry powder and top with a few baby shrimp (fresh or canned) or crab meat. Decorate with a sprinkle of paprika and a leaf of parsley.

FAST NO-COOK CANAPÉS II

Slice cored pears into one-quarter-inch slices and put a very thin slice of mozzarella cheese on top. Sprinkle with a sparing dash of cinnamon and decorate with a walnut half.

FAST NO-COOK CANAPÉS III

Use fresh fruit instead of a platter of raw vegetables. Cut pineapple, apple, peach, pear, nectarine, or melon into bite-size pieces. Dip fruit for a moment into water with several tablespoons of lemon juice so the fruit won't darken. Spear fruit with picks and arrange attractively on a platter covered generously with greens such as cress, parsley, or lettuce to heighten color contrast.

For the fruit dip: blend one cup mayonnaise with one and one-half tablespoons honey and one tablespoon lemon juice. Add drained crushed pineapple to taste.

FAST NO-COOK CANAPÉS IV

This one requires the purchase of an apple sectioner. It is small, practical, inexpensive and sold with the kitchen gadgets in most hardware stores and supermarkets. When pressed down through an apple, it not only cores and sections it in one fast movement but also holds the apple in an attractive fashion as a server while guests pick off the apple sections.

Use a small wood chopping block as a platter. On it put one or two wedges of cheese with a knife so guests can cut their own pieces, and a little pile of shelled nuts. Push the apple sectioner through the apple immediately before serving so the apple will not have time to discolor. Incidentally, Golden Delicious apples are slower to discolor than any other variety. Remove the core, which will have been cut by the sectioner, and serve the apple while still in the sectioner.

QUICK DIP

Thaw a box of frozen peas and the same quantity of frozen onions. Then purée them together until smooth. Serve with raw vegetables or crackers.

MY FAVORITE DIP

1 8-ounce package cream cheese
¼ cup mayonnaise
⅛ cup ketchup

1½ tablespoon honey
1 medium onion, quartered
2 teaspoons curry powder

Put all in blender and process until smooth.

MY FAVORITE LOW-CALORIE DIP

1 cup (8 ox.) large-curd cottage
   cheese
½ cup sour cream
3 tablespoons chopped chives
2 tablespoons parsley

1 garlic clove, crushed
½ teaspoon salt
1 teaspoon Worcestershire sauce
¼ teaspoon bottled red pepper
   sauce

Put all in blender and process until smooth. Refrigerate at least 2 hours.

Kissing don't last; cookery do.
GEORGE MEREDITH, 1859

CHAPTER TWO

Sauce . . .
Soup

SAUCE MADE EASY

When you have a little meat or chicken stock and want to make a simple sauce, do you know how to get the right consistency without trial and error? Just remember the formula 1–1–1. To thicken *one* cup of stock use *one* tablespoon butter and *one* tablespoon flour.

HOW TO MAKE A CLOUDY SAUCE BEAUTIFUL

Sauces made with fish stock are often gray in color. To make the sauce golden and creamy stir in two egg yolks combined with two tablespoons of heavy cream.

NO-STICK SAUCE

Did you know that a sauce prepared in a pan that has been rinsed in cold water is less apt to stick than one that is made in a dry pan?

HOW TO REDUCE YOUR TIME REDUCING A SAUCE

You do not have to stand over a sauce while it is reducing. Put it in the oven at 350° and let it reduce slowly by itself. Depending on the quantity, it may take from fifteen minutes to an hour. Experiment with it. This tip really works.

MEASURING LIQUID REDUCTION

Here is a foolproof way to measure how much your liquid has reduced. Put the handle of a wooden spoon upright in the liquid. Take it out and mark the level of the liquid with a pencil. Return the spoon.

As the liquid boils down, you can keep track of just how much the liquid is reducing.

FAT-FREE SAUCES I

To remove the fat from the surface of a sauce, put the pan half on and half off the source of heat. The fat will drift to the cooler side and can be lifted off easily with a shallow-bowled spoon.

FAT-FREE SAUCES II

When you want to remove the fat from a sauce, soup, or stock, pour the sauce into a tall narrow jar. The fat will rise quickly to the top and the narrow opening will make it easier to spoon out the fat.

FAT-FREE SAUCES III

Spread a paper towel over the surface of the sauce. The fat will cling to the towel. You can then remove the towel with a spatula.

FAT-FREE SAUCES IV

When your soup, sauce, or stock is still on the fire and you want to get rid of the fat, wrap three or four ice cubes in a dampened cloth or dish towel and, clenching it tightly, skim it over the surface of the liquid. The fat will cling to the cloth.

FAT-FREE SAUCES V

If you have time, put the fatty liquid in the refrigerator and chill for four hours. The fat will rise to the surface and harden. It can then be lifted off easily.

GRAVY SECRET

This secret is a great timesaver. Freeze leftover gravy in an ice-cube tray. Wrap solidly frozen gravy cubes in freezer wrap. Then when you need some gravy, reheat a cube or two.

NO-LUMP GRAVY

The trick is to use flour that has been browned. It not only makes the gravy taste better and gives it a richer color, but also helps to keep lumps from forming. The easy way to brown your flour is to put a little in a heat-proof dish when you're using the oven and leave it there until the flour has turned a nice brown color. Store it in the refrigerator in a jar until you are ready to use it.

IF YOU DO NOT HAVE GRAVY BROWNER

Use a little of that coffee left over from breakfast. Add just enough to give the gravy the rich brown color everyone likes. Two or three tablespoons of coffee will probably be sufficient. Surprisingly, the gravy will not taste of coffee.

BETTER COLOR FOR CHICKEN SAUCE

If your chicken soup or sauce doesn't have that rich golden chicken color, add a drop or two of yellow food coloring. It won't improve the taste, but the eye will be better satisfied.

HOMEMADE MAYONNAISE SECRET

When making mayonnaise by hand, mix the egg yolks and oil in a warm bowl. Add a teaspoon of dry or prepared mustard to the yolks before adding oil. This will reduce the risk of separation—the bane of all mayonnaise makers.

ADDING OIL DROP BY DROP

Oil must be added one drop at a time when you commence adding it to the egg yolk-mustard mixture. To make it easier, use a bulb baster instead of a spoon to add the oil drop by drop.

HOW TO UNCURDLE HOMEMADE MAYONNAISE

Sometimes homemade mayonnnaise curdles while you are making it. This is usually caused by having added the oil too quickly or because the oil has been cold and the egg yolks warm. The remedy is the same in either case. Put an egg yolk in a bowl and very slowly add the curdled mayonnaise a tablespoon at a time. Beat rapidly with a wire whisk and the mayonnaise will become smooth. As you progress, you can increase the speed at which the curdled mayonnaise is added.

MAKING STORE-BOUGHT MAYONNAISE TASTE ALMOST LIKE HOMEMADE

Simply add 1 tablespoon of good quality olive oil and one egg yolk to each cup of mayonnaise and stir thoroughly. What a difference!

CHAMPAGNE SAUCE WITHOUT CHAMPAGNE

When the recipe calls for champagne and you don't have any, or the funds to buy it, make do with dry white wine mixed with a little club soda. Use a two-thirds wine, one-third soda mixture.

HOW TO KEEP YOUR HOLLANDAISE FROM DISASTER

When you must make your hollandaise sauce ahead of time and you do not want to risk having it curdle when you reheat it, try this. Take one tablespoon of cornstarch and stir it into two tablespoons of cold milk. Then add one tablespoon of this mixture to every three egg yolks in the hollandaise. Add to the finished sauce. This trick is often used in restaurants.

HOW TO SERVE HOLLANDAISE WITHOUT HAVING TO MAKE IT AT THE LAST MINUTE

To keep hollandaise hot when it is made ahead of time, store it in a preheated thermos jug. It will keep warm for four hours with no risk of curdling. This is an excellent trick, and ensures a perfect sauce.

YET ANOTHER HOLLANDAISE SAUCE SECRET

If you add hot hollandaise, Béarnaise, or similar emulsified sauce to very hot foods, the combined heat may cause the sauce to separate. Let all emulsified sauces cool to room temperature before putting them on top of very hot steaks or other hot food.

HOW TO TAKE OUT PART OF THE LIQUID FROM THE POT

Sometimes there is too much liquid in a pot or casserole and you do not want to strain it from one pot to another. Here is a way of getting rid of some of the liquid without removing the pan from the heat. Sink a large strainer into the liquid, pressing down on the solid ingredients. Use a ladle to lift out the clear liquid that rises on top of the strainer.

HOW TO THICKEN A SAUCE AT THE LAST MINUTE

To thicken a sauce at the last minute, blend together equal amounts of butter and flour. You can do this in the palm of your hand. Start with two teaspoons of softened butter and use your thumb to work in two teaspoons of flour. Add a speck of the mixture at a time to the hot sauce and stir it into the sauce with a wire whisk. The sauce will thicken immediately. Sauces can also be thickened by stirring in cornstarch dissolved in cold water. Start with 1 tablespoon of cornstarch stirred into two tablespoons of cold water.

HOW TO THICKEN A FRUIT SAUCE

Purée soft fruit or berries in a food processor using the steel blade. Heat the purée and stir in one tablespoon of cornstarch or arrowroot dissolved in two tablespoons of cold water. Add this mixture a little at a time until the correct thickness is achieved. The sauce will be shiny and clear, not opaque.

HOW TO PREVENT A SKIN FROM FORMING ON SAUCE

To prevent a skin from forming on a completed sauce, cover the surface of the sauce with a thin film of melted butter. When the sauce is reheated the butter will melt into the sauce. If the sauce is made ahead of time, cover it with transparent wrap to exclude the air completely.

REHEATING SOUP

When you have made a large quantity of soup in advance, reheat only the quantity that you anticipate will be eaten. Soups that contain meats, chicken, fish, vegetables, and either rice or pasta will be over-cooked if they are reheated two or three times.

CANNED BOUILLON

To remove the excess sweetness from canned beef bouillon or broth, simmer it for five minutes with a small amount of chopped onion, garlic, and celery. Do not add carrots. It is the carrots that make it too sweet. Strain out vegetables before serving.

COLD SOUP

All food when cold loses saltiness. Add more salt to cold soups such as vichyssoise when necessary.

FREEZING SOUP

Almost all homemade soups can be frozen. The only exceptions are those made with egg yolks, cream, or potatoes. Tomato soup also has a tendency to separate when it is frozen.

Some of the taste is lost when soup is frozen. Perk it up with additional salt, pepper, and herbs.

GOOD FREEZING CONTAINERS

Save quart or one-half-gallon milk or juice containers. Freeze soup in them. They will stack neatly in the freezer and save lots of space. They're free, too.

A little kitchen makes a large house.
HERBERT, 1640

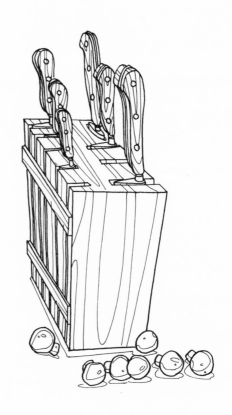

CHAPTER THREE

Meat . . .
Poultry

HOW TO KEEP THE MEAT JUICES IN

Do not salt a roast until it is half done. Do not salt steak or hamburger until both sides have been cooked.

HOW TO GET THE MEAT JUICES OUT

When you make a broth or soup, you want the juices to flow freely from the meat. The secret is to put the meat in cold water. Bring it slowly to a boil and then continue to simmer it slowly. The juices will be released. Hot liquid seals the meat and keeps the juices trapped.

IF YOU DO NOT HAVE A CROCK POT I

You can still get that slow cooked flavor and convenience. Put all your stew ingredients in a covered casserole and cook it for eight hours in a 200° oven.

IF YOU DO NOT HAVE A CROCK POT II

Put a couple of bricks on top of a low gas flame. Set your pot of soup or stew on top of the bricks and simmer slowly all day or all night.

HOW TO BRAISE WITHOUT BOILING I

Braised meat has a glorious flavor, but too often meat that is intended to be braised becomes boiled; the end result tastes like stew. To get that wonderful rich taste in a pot roast or braised veal, cook your meat in a heavy pan with a tightly fitting lid and a minimum of liquid, not more than 1 cup of liquid to 4 pounds of meat. Use the shallowest pan you have so there will be very little space between the meat and the lid for steam to accumulate.

HOW TO BRAISE WITHOUT BOILING II

When you do not have a small enough pan for the size of your meat, place a piece of foil shaped like a saucer over the top of the meat. The condensation that gathers on the lid will then fall onto your foil plate instead of onto the meat. There will not be any steam to give the meat that boiled taste.

NEW TASTE FOR STEW

Add a teaspoon or two of freeze-dried coffee to your stew. It will not only give it an interesting, though not identifiable flavor, but will also give the stew a dark, rich brown color.

TASTY WAY TO SAVE COOKING TIME

Did you know that marinating meat overnight reduces cooking time by almost half? You will save time and energy, and have a more flavorful dish as well.

IF YOU DO NOT HAVE A MEAT TENDERIZER I

There is more than one way to tame a tough cut of beef. Cook it in strong tea or in beer instead of using water. The tannin in the tea or the alcohol in the beer will tenderize the meat.

IF YOU DO NOT HAVE A MEAT TENDERIZER II

Cook the meat with a lot of tomatoes. The acidity in the tomatoes will break down the tough meat fibers.

IF YOU DO NOT HAVE A MEAT TENDERIZER III

A tough piece of round steak can be made tender by marinating it in two cups of cold water and one tablespoon of vinegar for thirty minutes. Turn the steak after fifteen minutes.

HOW TO OIL A ROAST

The easiest way to oil a roast is to spray it with a vegetable oil that comes in a spray can. These cans are usually found either in the baking section of the supermarket or with the vegetable and olive oils. Or you could put your favorite oil into a spray bottle kept especially for this purpose.

HOW TO ROAST WHEN YOU DO NOT HAVE A RACK

If you do not have a roasting rack and you want to keep the underside of the meat from frying in its own fat, use two or three metal jar lids with holes punched in the tops. The roast will be perfectly happy sitting on top of the punched lids and the hot dry air in the oven will be able to circulate freely.

HOW TO HANDLE ROAST MEATS

When you remove a roast from the oven, let it stand for fifteen minutes to allow the juices to reassemble. This will make carving easier and the meat will be moist and flavorful. Do not attempt to cook a roast smaller than three pounds in weight. It becomes dry before it is fully cooked.

ROASTING TEMPERATURES

The suggested temperatures on many charts and thermometers are usually too high and if followed give you meat that is overcooked. Use a thin thermometer that gives an instant reading for the greatest accuracy. The correct temperatures are:

Beef and Lamb	Rare	100–115 °F.
	Medium rare	115–120 °F.
	Medium	120–130 °F.
Veal		cook to 155 °F.
Pork		cook to 160 °F.
Chicken, duck, turkey		cook to 175 °F.

When finished let the roast stand for 15 minutes. The interior temperature will continue to rise up to 10° F. as the heat distributes.

TO KEEP YOUR STEAK FLAT

To prevent steak from curling, cut several nicks in the fat all around the piece of meat.

HOW TO TELL WHEN THE STEAK IS DONE

Don't cut the meat. Use your finger. Imagine how raw meat feels. Now, press the hot meat purposefully with your finger. Rare meats give a little. Medium meat is firmer and more resistant. Well-done meat is very firm. This method takes a little practice, but if a professional chef can do it, so can you.

HOW TO AVOID A FAT FIRE IN THE BROILER

Simply place slices of bread under the rack to catch the drippings. This will prevent a fat flare-up.

HOW TO BROIL THIN SLICES OF MEAT

If you broil thin pieces of meat, you can prevent them from drying out by dipping them first in flour, then in egg yolks combined with milk—one egg yolk to one tablespoon of milk—and finally dredging the meat in fine breadcrumbs. The meat will remain moist and have a delicious crisp coating.

HOW TO FRY MEAT

Dry meats on paper towels before frying or they will not brown. Do not salt meat before frying. The salt will cause the blood to rise to the surface and the juices will be lost in the hot fat. The meat will become dry and stringy and stick to the pan. Wait until the meat is turned before salting.

HOW TO TELL WHEN TO TURN THE MEAT

When broiling or frying, the meat is ready to be turned when droplets of blood rise to the surface.

HOW TO SLICE RAW MEAT PAPER THIN

When you need paper-thin slices of raw beef, chicken, or pork, put it in the freezer for about an hour or until it is firm but not completely frozen. It is then easy to cut tissue-thin slices for Oriental cooking or stroganoff with any sharp knife.

HOW TO WORK WITH GROUND MEAT

If you handle ground meat too much it becomes heavy and compacted. It will also stay lighter and juicier if you add a tablespoon or two of cold water or red wine to each pound of ground meat.

Wet your hands with cold water when making meat balls or hamburger patties. The meat will then not stick to your hands. Ground meat should be eaten within two days of its purchase.

HAMBURGER SECRET WHEN THERE'S A CROWD

Here is a quick and fair way to divide hamburger for a large group. Use an ice-cream scoop for a measure. The patties will be of uniform size, and you'll get the job done faster.

FROZEN MEAT-BALL CONTAINER

Freeze meat balls in an egg carton lined with transparent wrap. Put one meatball in each compartment. Cover the entire carton with aluminum foil. The result: easy-to-stack boxes and easy-to-thaw individual meat balls.

A TASTIER MEAT LOAF I

To obtain a better distribution of spices when you're making a meat loaf, mix spices with a little water or a lightly beaten egg before adding to the meat.

Experiment with different spices. For one pound of meat try adding:

- 1 to 2 tablespoons horseradish
- or ¼ cup chopped mixed parsley, basil, and chives
- or 2 tablespoons soy sauce, or ¼ cup Taco sauce and ¼ cup crumbled corn chips
- or 2 teaspoons curry powder
- or 2 teaspoons chili powder.

Add a cup of chopped apples, ½ cup raisins, a little mango chutney, and spice with curry powder for an Indian-type meal. Or use 1 cup sliced water chestnuts and soy sauce for an Oriental type dish.

A TASTIER MEAT LOAF II

Meat loaves and pâtés taste better if made from two or three meats, such as veal, ham and pork, or beef, rather than a single meat. Not only do flavors enhance each other, but there is a difference in texture.

A FLUFFIER MEAT LOAF

Add a pinch (about ½ teaspoon) of baking powder to the meat mixture before baking. You will be amazed at the difference in the texture of the loaf—lighter.

MEAT LOAF MADE IN UNDER FIFTEEN MINUTES

Yes, it is possible! When time is a factor, form the meat into several small loaves and bake them in miniature foil bread pans. Small loaves will be fully cooked in fifteen minutes.

HOW TO STORE MEAT

Remove meat and poultry from transparent supermarket wrapping to allow it to breathe. Wrap loosely in wax paper or foil before storing to increase its refrigerator life.

FREEZER BURN ON MEAT

There will be less chance of freezer burn if you put a thin coat of vegetable oil on the surface of meat before wrapping securely.

SEPARATING BACON SLICES

One of the most frustrating things about bacon is trying to separate thin slices. Here's the secret. Roll the entire package crosswise before you open it. You will find that the bacon slices will separate in an instant.

HOW TO KEEP YOUR BACON STRAIGHT

To help prevent bacon from curling while frying, put it in a cold pan and cook it slowly, or bake it on a rack in a preheated 325°F. oven. Be sure there is a drip pan beneath the oven rack.

WHEN YOU'RE A PIG ABOUT BACON

When you have too much bacon, more than the pan will hold, crisscross the slices and turn all at one time with a pancake turner or a wide spatula.

WHAT TO DO WITH LEFTOVER BACON

Crumble leftover bacon and use it for garnishing soups, salads, and vegetables.

SAVE ON PAPER TOWELS

At today's prices, paper towels cost as much as steak did in the good old days. But there is at least one way to economize: instead of using several thicknesses of paper towel to drain bacon, or other fried food, use only one layer of paper toweling placed on top of several layers of newspaper.

HOW TO AVOID A SOGGY MEAT-PIE CRUST

Steam and gravy have a tendency to make the top crust of a meat pie soggy. You can avoid this by brushing the underside of the crust thoroughly with egg white before cooking, making sure every inch is completely covered. Then prick air holes with a fork on the top crust so the steam can escape. Of course, if you want to be absolutely certain the crust will not become soggy, bake it separately on a cookie sheet and lay it on top of the pie immediately before serving.

HOW TO MAKE "MOCK" VEAL DISHES

Use boned and skinned chicken breasts instead of veal for many dishes such as veal parmigiana or veal scallopini. The chicken will taste almost as good as the veal and some claim that it is even better. The important thing is to pound the chicken so it is very thin. Lay the chicken breasts between two pieces of wax paper and pound them with the side of a cleaver or with the bottom of a heavy iron pan.

BEAUTY TREATMENT FOR VEAL

Did you know that if you soak veal overnight in milk, or for thirty minutes sprinkled with lemon juice, it will become snowy white?

IF YOU DON'T LIKE THE SMELL OF LAMB

If you like the taste of lamb, but don't like the odor—particularly when it is cooking—remove all the lamb fat before you cook it. Much of the lamb odor comes from the fat.

HOW MUCH LAMB TO BUY

When buying a leg of lamb, approximately one-third of the weight will be bone. So, a six-pound leg of lamb will yield approximately four pounds of meat. Allow one-third to one-half pound of lamb for each person for lamb cooked without the bone. With the bone in allow one-half to three-quarters pound of meat per person.

HOW TO COOK LIVER

Remove all blood vessels and other pieces of unpleasantness from liver before cooking. Use embroidery or nail scissors. When cooking liver, cut two or three notches around the edge of each slice to prevent it from curling as the surrounding membrane contracts with the heat.

ROAST CHICKEN WITH A CRISPER SKIN

There are two ways to crisp chicken skin: either roast the chicken in a preheated 450°F. oven or rub mayonnaise (of all things!) on the skin and cook it at the usual 375°F. temperature.

BETTER FLAVOR FOR CHICKEN

You will get a better flavor from your chicken or Cornish hen if you put herb-flavored butter between the skin and the meat of the bird. Run your finger beneath the skin to loosen it and spread the butter on the meat. Butter flavored with tarragon or garlic is particularly appetizing.

HOW TO MAKE SURE FRIED CHICKEN PARTS ARE EVENLY COOKED

When frying chicken, start with the legs and add the breasts a few minutes later. Dark meat takes longer to cook than white meat.

HOW TO MAKE SURE ROASTED POULTRY IS EVENLY COOKED

Truss chicken and other poultry before roasting or the wings and thighs will be overcooked.

HOW TO MAKE MOIST CHICKEN FOR SALADS

A chicken for salad or sandwiches will be flavorful and moist if you poach it in chicken broth. Simply put chicken into hot broth and simmer for twenty minutes. Turn off the heat and let stand tightly covered for another twenty minutes.

CHICKEN CASSEROLE SECRET

When chicken is cooked in a casserole, the leg meat shrinks, exposing the bone. For a more attractive appearance, trim off the bone ends and wing tips using a poultry shears.

CHICKEN BARBECUE SECRET

I wish I had a dime for every chicken barbecued on an outdoor grill that was undercooked in the center. Often the chicken is nice and brown on the outside—even burned—yet completely raw on the inside. To avoid this, use small broilers, under two pounds in weight. Cut the chicken into quarters, or ask the butcher to cut it in half and remove the backbone, so it will lie flat and be of uniform thickness. The chicken will then cook evenly. Cook with the cavity side down for three-quarters of the estimated cooking time, then turn it and continue cooking for the remaining time. Make sure it is completely cooked before serving by cutting into a piece. The juice should run clear, not reddish.

BREAST-BONING SECRET

When boning a chicken breast, be sure to remove the white tendon or it will contract during cooking, causing the chicken meat to shrink.

DRESSING FOR POULTRY

Do not put dressing in the poultry cavity until you are ready to cook it. Dressing deteriorates rapidly in this environment. Do not pack too tightly. Dressing expands as it cooks and it may erupt from the cavity and the dressing in the center of the cavity may become so densely packed that heat cannot reach it.

HOW TO DEFROST A DUCK

It takes six hours to defrost a duck at room temperature. A better way is to defrost it slowly in the refrigerator where it will take up to twelve hours to thaw.

HOW TO COOK A DUCK

Prick the duck skin all over with a fork to allow the fat to drain freely. Prick before cooking and every thirty minutes. Even though duck is extremely fatty, you will not be able to get a crisp brown skin unless you rub the surface of the bird with butter. To achieve a dark, almost black color rub the duck skin with butter and honey combined in equal parts. Always cook a duck on a roasting rack to allow the fat to drain.

HOW TO CHOOSE A ROASTING PAN

A shiny aluminum roasting pan reflects the heat and can add as much as twenty-five minutes to the total cooking time of a chicken. During this extra time the chicken often becomes dry and stringy. Dark aluminum pans, on the other hand, absorb the heat and when the chicken is fully cooked it is moist, the skin is crisp and has a good color.

SECRET TO BETTER BATTER FRYING

If you want batter to cling to your meat, chicken, fish, or vegetables make sure the ingredient to be fried is completely dry. Dredge it with flour before dipping it in the batter.

CHICKEN LIVERS THAT WON'T FIGHT BACK

Chicken livers often "explode" when they are cooked over too high a heat. You can prevent this by pricking them with a fork before cooking and cooking them over moderate heat.

HOW TO CHEAT LIKE A CHEF

When a chef makes a pâté en croute, you never see a space between the meat and the crust, even though the meat shrinks as it cooks. A chef waits until the pâté has cooled completely and then pours aspic that is almost at the point of setting through a hole in the top crust. The aspic will fill the space completely when it has set.

HOW TO PREVENT BRATWURST AND OTHER SAUSAGES FROM SPLATTERING

To prevent bratwurst and similar sausages from squirting in your face when you eat them, hold the sausage steady with your fork and cut it immediately behind—not in front of—the fork.

If a man will be sensible and one fine morning, while he is lying in bed, count at the tips of his fingers how many things in his life truly give him enjoyment, invariably he will find food is the first one.

LIN YUTANG

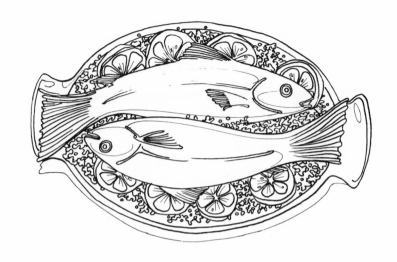

CHAPTER FOUR

Fish . . .
    Shellfish

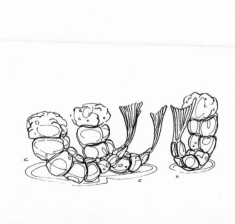

HOW MUCH FISH TO BUY

For four people buy:

1½ pounds boneless filleted fish
2 pounds fish steaks or cutlets
3 pounds whole fish with head and tail removed
4 pounds whole fish with the head and tail intact

HOW LONG TO POACH FISH

Whole fish under two pounds, cook for ten minutes to the pound.

Whole fish under five pounds, cook for eight minutes to the pound.

Whole fish over five pounds, cook for six minutes to the pound.

HOW TO SKIN A FISH

To remove the skin from raw fish, start at the tail end. Hold the tail firmly in one hand. With a thin, flexible bladed knife use a sawing motion. With the blade held almost parallel to the counter, work your way toward the head. Reserve the skin and bones for a fish broth to use as the basis for a fish sauce.

REMOVING SMALL BONES FROM RAW FISH

The most effective way of finding hidden bones in uncooked fish is to run your fingertips from the head down to the tail. Remove small bones with your fingers or with eyebrow tweezers.

HOW TO KEEP YOUR FISH WHOLE

Nothing is more frustrating than to poach a large whole fish to perfection and then to have it break when you are transferring it to the serving dish. The secret is to put it on a large piece of greased foil or parchment paper *before* you add the liquid and cook it. Make sure the paper or foil extends over the edges of the pan. When the fish is cooked, hold the foil or parchment paper taut as you take the fish out of the pan and slide it onto the serving dish.

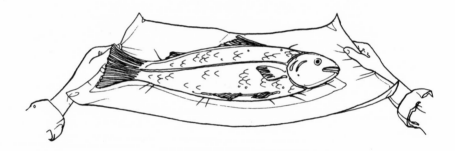

HOW TO PREVENT BAKED FISH FROM STICKING TO THE PAN

Baked fish or frozen fish sticks won't adhere to the pan if you line it with crumpled aluminum foil before baking. Crumpled foil works much better than smooth because less of the food rests on the foil.

POACHING HINT I

Place the fish in a greased pan (to prevent sticking) and then add cold liquid. Hot liquid will cause the skin to rupture.

POACHING HINT II

A whole fish has a better chance of staying in one piece if you let it cool completely in the liquid in which it was cooked.

IF YOU DON'T HAVE A POACHING PAN

Use your largest roasting pan.

HOW TO SKIN A COOKED FISH

Drain poached fish on a wire cake-cooling rack. To remove the skin, make a cut down the center of the back of the fish and peel off the skin while the fish is still warm.

MASTERING THE THICK FILLET

To keep fish from being overcooked and dry, or undercooked and raw, squeeze the juice of half a lemon over the fish and leave it to marinate for twenty minutes. The acid of the lemon partially "cooks" the fish and then you can cook a thick fillet as you would a normal-size fillet.

HOW TO TELL WHEN THE FISH IS COMPLETELY COOKED

This is a foolproof method. Insert a thin metal skewer into the fish and leave it there for thirty seconds. Test the skewer on your wrist. If it is only warm, cook the fish for two or three more minutes. If the skewer is evenly hot, the fish is ready.

ANOTHER WAY TO TELL IF THE FISH IS READY

To test whether fish is cooked, use a sharp knife to flake it near the bone. If there is any visible blood, continue cooking the fish for another two or three minutes. If the flesh is white and opaque and flakes easily, it is cooked sufficiently.

PERFECT BROILED FISH

Grease your broiling pan or rack *after* it has been heated. The hotter the pan is before the fish goes on it, the better textured will be the underside of the fish, and it won't stick to the pan.

PERFECTLY CRISP FRIED FISH

If you want your fried fish to have a beautiful crisp coating, the fat in which you fry it must be very hot, 375°F. There must also be enough fat for the fish to easily slide around in the pan. Not great for the figure, but, oh, so tasty.

NO-COOK METHOD TO "COOK" SEAFOOD

Lemon juice gives fish more than a tangy taste, it also makes a firmer texture as the acidity of the juice slightly "cooks" the fish. Scallops, for example, if left overnight in lemon or lime juice do not need to be cooked and are delicious in a seafood cocktail.

DON'T LET FRIED FISH GET BALD SPOTS

After you dredge fish in flour and breadcrumbs, be sure the fish is completely covered and there are no bald spots. Otherwise the fat will get between the breading and the skin and the coating will become detached. This secret applies to all fried foods.

FRYING DO'S AND DON'TS I

Chill food thoroughly before frying. The fibers should be tightly contracted so the fat cannot penetrate into the food itself. Use two forks to dip foods in egg and breadcrumb coating and into batters. This is less messy than using your fingers.

FRYING DO'S AND DON'TS II

Do not dredge foods in flour, breadcrumbs, or batter until you are ready to cook them or the coating will become soggy.

FRYING DO'S AND DON'TS III

Do not fill deep-fat-frying pans more than half full or the fat will spill over the edge when the food is added.

FRYING DO'S AND DON'TS IV

Do not crowd foods that are being deep-fried. The foods will steam, the steam will condense into the fat and make it waterlogged, preventing the food from becoming crisp and brown.

FRYING DO'S AND DON'TS V

Do not use a deep-frying wire basket when frying small foods such as batter-fried shrimp. The shrimp get trapped between the wires and they are difficult to remove.

HOW TO GET RID OF FISH ODORS

To eliminate lingering kitchen odors after a fish has been cooked, boil a small amount of vinegar. It works wonders. To remove the fish smell from clay pots and other pans, scrub them with baking soda and rinse with white vinegar. Another method is to boil a tablespoon or two of vinegar in water in the pan before washing it.

UNMOLDING A FISH MOUSSE

If you wait for a few minutes before removing a hot fish mousse from its mold you will find that it shrinks a little as it cools. When you turn it over, it will slide from the mold more easily.

MASTERING THE SEAFOOD QUENELLE

Although fish or seafood quenelles are correctly described as "featherlike dumplings," to do so does them an injustice. Once eaten they are never forgotten. However, until the invention of the food processor they were almost impossible for the homemaker to make. Now it is a cinch to process fish or seafood until it is a smooth paste. The only hard part is to mold the mixture into neat ovals. You do that with two tablespoons. The secret is to have one tablespoon hot and wet and the other cold and wet. So, keep two bowls of water nearby—one hot and the other cold. Scoop out a generous amount of the quenelle mixture with the cold tablespoon, use the hot spoon to shape the mixture and slide it from the cold spoon.

HOW TO SEPARATE LEAN FISH FROM FAT FISH

Fish are classified as either lean or fat. Lean fish are usually fried, sautéed in butter, poached, or steamed. In other words they are cooked in some form of liquid. Fatty fish are best cooked by dry heat; they can be baked, broiled, or cooked over charcoal.

Lean fish are served with buttery sauces and fatty fish are best accompanied with tomato sauce and vegetable garnishings.

Lean fish:

Bluefish	Perch
Cod	Pike
Croaker	Red snapper
Flounder	Shellfish (all)
Haddock	Sole
Hake	Swordfish
Halibut	Whiting
Herring	

Fat fish:

Butterfish	Salmon
Catfish	Smelt
Chub	Striped bass
Lake trout	Turbot
Pompano	Whitefish

FREEZING LARGE WHOLE FISH

If you have a whole fish of good size, put it in a large container such as a roasting pan filled with cold water and place it in the freezer. After about an hour take the fish from the water; the fish will be encased in a thin layer of ice. Put the frozen fish in a florist box and store it in the freezer.

HOW TO CHOOSE A LOBSTER

When buying a live lobster, find out how long it has been in the tank. Lobsters in captivity feed on themselves and the longer they have been in the tank, the less meat will be left for you. The weight of the lobster may be largely in the shell and not in the meat.

HOW MUCH LOBSTER TO BUY

A one and one-half pound lobster is usually sufficient for all but the greedy and the addicted. Lobsters are best when boiled or steamed for eighteen minutes. Few lobster connoisseurs deign to eat broiled lobsters because broiling causes lobsters to lose their juices and to be invariably dry.

HOW TO KEEP A LOBSTER LIVE

Keep live lobsters enclosed in the bag in which they are purchased. Put them in the refrigerator where in theory they can survive for twelve hours but rarely do. Cook them as soon as possible. If you leave them to frolic in a sink of fluorinated cold water they will surely drown. Fluoride, while beneficial for the teeth of small children, does nothing to prolong the life of a lobster.

HOW TO KILL A LOBSTER

To retain all the juice, kill a live lobster by inserting a sharp knife at the spot where the body meets the tail. Nature has drawn intersecting lines to mark the exact spot.

IF YOU ARE CHICKEN WHEN IT COMES TO LOBSTER

If you cannot bear to cook a live lobster, ask your friendly fishman to cook it for you. If you want to serve hot lobster, ask him to under-cook it by five or ten minutes. Then you will not run the risk of overcooking it when you reheat it at home. Incidentally, you can tell if the lobster was alive when it was cooked. A live lobster will have its tail tightly curled under its body after it is cooked.

IF YOU'RE NOT CHICKEN WHEN IT COMES TO LOBSTER

If you're courageous enough to boil the lobster yourself and you don't want the tail to curl while boiling, tie it to a wooden cooking spoon before lowering the lobster into the boiling water.

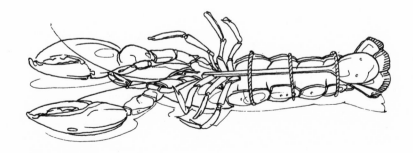

HOW TO DRAIN LOBSTERS

To remove the excess water from a boiled lobster, plunge the point of a sharp knife between the eyes and hold the lobster upside down to permit drainage.

HOW MUCH SHRIMP TO BUY

When buying shrimp still in the shell, double the quantity to allow for wastage. One pound of shrimp in the shell will serve three people. One pound of shelled shrimp will serve six.

HOW TO TENDERIZE A SEA SCALLOP

The large, plump sea scallops are considerably less expensive than the tiny bay scallops, but they are also less tender. You will never know the difference if you cut the sea scallops *across the grain*, into tiny pieces.

OYSTERS SHUCKED WITH EASE

Oysters too difficult for you to shuck? Try this. Put them into a 400°F. oven for about five minutes. Then drop them into ice water for exactly one minute. You will be delighted when you see how easily they can be opened. The oysters can then be made into oyster stew or stuffing or used in other cooked dishes. Once heated they are not good to serve on the half shell.

HOW TO OUTFOX A STUBBORN CLAM

When you have trouble removing a clam from its shell, drop it in boiling water for just a few seconds. Then use your knife to pry the shell open.

REMOVING SAND FROM CLAMS

If you want to make sure you have removed all the sand from clams, sprinkle them—still in their shell—with plenty of corn meal and then cover the clams with cold water. After thirty minutes all the sand should be out of the clams. *Lift* the clams out of the water, do not make the mistake of draining them in a strainer. Rinse in 2 changes of clean, cold water and they will be ready to cook.

LESS MUSCLE CLEANING MUSSELS

Use a nail brush to scrub raw mussels. The bristles are shorter and firmer than those on a vegetable brush and you can clean the mussels more efficiently.

SALTY ANCHOVIES

To remove the excess salt from anchovies, immerse them in milk for ten minutes. Drain off the milk and give it to the cat.

The reason it costs so much to live is that yesterday's luxuries are always becoming today's necessities.

CHAPTER FIVE

Vegetables . . .
Fruit

PERFECT BAKED POTATO

If you want a flakier potato, prick it with a fork half way through baking so the steam can escape.

TASTIER POTATO SKINS

Oil the skins of potatoes with bacon drippings before baking them. You'll love the flavor.

THE PAPER TRICK FOR POTATOES

Flakier boiled potatoes are easy to make with this treasured secret. Simply pour off all the water from potatoes after they are boiled and cover the pot with a double thickness of paper towels then cover with the saucepan lid. In ten minutes steam will be absorbed by the towels and your potatoes will be dry and flaky. The same secret works with rice.

BOILED POTATOES OLD AND NEW

Your great-grandmother knew this secret and you should too. Always start old boiling potatoes in *cold* water. Cook new potatoes in boiling salted water—or better yet, steam them in a vegetable steamer.

HOW TO KEEP BOILED POTATOES WHITE

Add a little milk to the water before boiling the potatoes. Not only will your potatoes remain snow white, they will taste better too.

QUICK MASHED POTATOES

In just a few minutes you can boil potatoes soft enough for mashing if you cut the raw potatoes with a french-fry cutter into small, even-sized pieces. Mashed potatoes cooked by this method don't take much more time than the boxed dried variety.

BE A SMASH WITH THE MASH

If you heat the milk or cream and butter before adding them to the potatoes, your mashed potatoes will remain hot and have a smoother, creamier texture.

If you do not plan to serve mashed potatoes immediately, put them in the top of a double boiler and keep them hot over a low flame with hot—not boiling—water in the bottom part of the double boiler.

PERFECTLY BROWNED POTATOES

Fried potatoes will brown evenly if you sprinkle them with a little flour before frying.

PERFECT FRENCH FRIES

First wrap the raw potatoes, cut up for frying, in an absorbent kitchen towel and chill them in the freezer for a half hour before cooking. This will keep them from splattering during frying. Then fry the potatoes in two stages. Fill a deep pan a little less than half full of oil or fat and heat it to 300°–315° (use a thermometer). Don't cook too many at one time—two handfuls is about right. Let the potatoes cook for two or three minutes, remove from fat, drain on paper towels and leave to cool. Heat oil or fat again—this time to 375° and fry potatoes another two or three minutes or until crisp and brown.

Drain them in a *single layer* on paper towels spread on wire cake-cooling racks. If you pile them, the steam will be trapped and they will become soggy. The same thing will happen if you cover them.

This method is not only foolproof, but is enormously helpful if you are preparing a company dinner, because the first frying process can be done early in the day.

GREAT GRATED POTATOES

Grate potatoes directly into a bowl of ice water to prevent them from turning brown. When ready to cook, wrap them in a kitchen towel and squeeze all the water from the potatoes. They will not become crisp and brown if they are wet.

HOW TO STORE HALF AN ONION

Onion will stay fresh and moist if it is stored in a covered jar in the refrigerator.

ONION JUICE

Try using onion juice instead of chopped onion when preparing a smooth sauce. I keep a small orange-juice squeezer just for this purpose. The onion need not be peeled to extract the juice and you will not have to strain the sauce as you would when you use chopped onion.

TIMESAVER WHEN PEELING ONIONS

When your recipe calls for a large amount of sliced onion, save yourself some tears and work. Buy large onions. After all it takes as much work to peel a small onion as a large one.

HOW TO SWEETEN AN ONION

If an onion is too strong-tasting, slice it and then soak it in cold water for thirty minutes.

IF ONIONS MAKE YOU CRY

Much of the juice in an onion is concentrated at the root end, so begin slicing the onion from this end and you will have fewer tears. Cold onions taken directly from the refrigerator will not make you cry as readily as onions that are at room temperature.

NOBODY LOVES A HAND THAT SMELLS OF ONION

After preparing onions, scrub your hands with salt before washing them and you will get rid of most of the odor. If an odor persists, rub parsley or celery leaves on your hands. Chew a little parsley to help cleanse your breath of onion odors.

Another way to rid your hands of onion odor: rinse your hands with rubbing alcohol. Be sure to follow this treatment with hand cream so there will not be any drying effect.

HOW TO LOVE A CANNED ONION

Canned onions sometimes taste tinny. Drain the onions, pour boiling salted water over them, and let them stand for a few minutes to remove that taste.

HOW TO KEEP SHALLOTS FRESH

Shallots will mold if there is too much moisture in the refrigerator. They will become shriveled if the surrounding air is too dry. To store shallots keep them in a sealed plastic bag in the refrigerator and they will create their own microclimate.

EASY WAY TO FIND A CLOVE OF GARLIC

Thread garlic cloves on toothpicks before putting into a casserole. The toothpicks can be seen and removed easily, whereas garlic cloves tend to become lost in dark gravies.

GARLIC-SKINNING SECRETS

To remove garlic skins quickly, drop the bulb into boiling water for a few seconds. The skins will pop off. Another way to remove skins faster is to whack each clove with a cleaver, jar bottom, or the side of a wide knife.

ANOTHER GARLIC SECRET

Before chopping garlic, sprinkle the cloves with salt. The salt will pick up the juice that is otherwise left on the chopping board.

HOW TO AVOID GARLIC HANDS

No matter how much we love garlic, nobody wants to have hands that constantly smell of garlic. The way to avoid "garlic hands" is to make a garlic purée once a week, or once a month, depending on the amount of garlic you customarily expect to use. Use an entire garlic bulb each time and purée it by mashing with a knife or in a food processor using the steel blade. Put the garlic paste in a small jar and stir in a tablespoon of vegetable or olive oil to keep the mixture moist. One-quarter teaspoon of the purée is equivalent to a clove of whole garlic. The garlic purée will remain fresh for about five weeks.

ANOTHER GARLIC SECRET

When you want crushed garlic and you don't have a garlic press, here's an easy method. Put your garlic cloves between two sheets of waxed paper and roll them with a rolling pin. The side of a knife can also be used, but a rolling pin is quicker. All the juice will stay inside the waxed paper and there will be no waste and no cleanup.

HOW TO OUTSMART A LIMA

Lima beans are a lot easier to shell if you cut a little sliver from the inside edge of the pod.

HOW TO TELL IF DRIED BEANS ARE COOKED

When you are boiling dried beans you don't need to keep sampling them to see if they are fully cooked. Simply take one out of the pot, blow on it and if the skin pops, the beans are ready. Saves time, calories, and your appetite.

WHEN COOKING CORN PASS UP THE SALT

Put the corn in a pan with a pinch of sugar and just enough cold water to cover. Don't put salt into the water or the corn will toughen. When water is at the boiling point toss in a teaspoon or two of salt. Drain *immediately* and the corn will be cooked tender and ready to eat. You don't need to time it or test it. If you start with cold water it will be cooked properly when the water is boiling.

HOW TO REMOVE CORN SILK

Corn silk is a nuisance, but you can get rid of it easily by running a damp paper towel over the shucked ear.

HOW TO KEEP STUFFED GREEN PEPPER FROM COLLAPSING

Bake stuffed peppers in greased muffin tins. The tins will give them some support as they cook. The same trick can be used when making stuffed onions or tomatoes.

HOW TO PEEL A GREEN PEPPER

Some people cannot digest cooked pepper skins, so it is best to peel them before they are cooked. Put the peppers under a preheated broiler for just a few moments. Then drop them immediately into a paper bag. Close the bag tightly. The steam from the heat of the peppers will loosen the skins and they can be slipped off easily.

KEEP THE GREEN IN GREEN PEAS AND BEANS

Keep green vegetables from turning dark by cooking in an uncovered pan. Adding one-half teaspoon of lemon juice helps too. Be careful not to overcook green peas and beans. If the vegetables are not to be eaten immediately, drain them in a colander and rinse them under cold running water. The color will brighten at once. To reheat, plunge them into boiling water for a minute or two or sauté them in hot butter.

KEEP WHITE VEGETABLES WHITE

Keep white vegetables from turning yellow when they are boiled by adding one-half teaspoon of cream of tartar to the boiling salted water.

ASPARAGUS TIPS

Wrap fresh asparagus in wet paper towels and then store in the vegetable keeper in the refrigerator.

Do not soak asparagus in water or much of the flavor will be lost. However, do be sure asparagus are well washed to remove any lingering grains of sand.

Try peeling asparagus with a cheese slicer. This is easier than using either a potato peeler or a paring knife.

If you do not have an asparagus steamer, tie bunches of asparagus with thin string and stand them in a pot with the lower third of the stems immersed in water. Cover the pan with another—inverted—saucepan to create a tall saucepan. The two saucepans should, of course, have matching diameters to create a steamer effect.

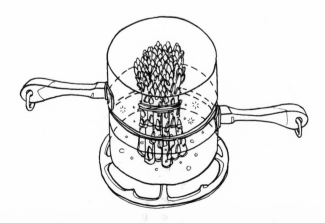

HOW TO PEEL A CELERY KNOB

First cut the celery knob into slices, then peel. In this way the bumps and projections will be easier to remove.

HOW TO MASH A PUMPKIN WITH NO STRINGS ATTACHED

Mash your golden pumpkin with an electric mixer. The pumpkin strings will wrap themselves around the mixing arm, leaving a smooth pumpkin purée.

HOW TO BUY AN EGGPLANT WITH FEWER SEEDS

The fewer seeds in an eggplant, the less bitter it tastes. There is a way to tell, before you cut into it, which eggplant has the fewest seeds. Check the bottom—the end opposite the stem. There you will find a greyish "scar" or indentation about the size of a dime. If the "scar" is oval or oblong the eggplant will be loaded with seeds. Choose the one with the round "scar" and you will have an eggplant with far fewer seeds.

SECRET OF REHEATING VEGETABLES

Food should be brought to room temperature before reheating. The fastest way to reheat vegetables is to stir-fry them in a wok using a teaspoon or two of peanut oil.

FIRST AID FOR WILTED LETTUCE

If your salad greens become limp, bring them back to life by washing them in—of all things—hot water. Then plunge them into ice water with a tablespoon or two of added vinegar. The lettuce will perk up dramatically.

EASY-DRY LETTUCE FOR A CROWD

When you will be serving salad to a large group, put all the washed lettuce leaves into a clean pillowcase. Tie the open end and put the filled pillowcase into the washing machine set at spin dry. Spin for a few moments and the lettuce will be absolutely dry. To toss the salad, put greens into a large plastic garbage bag, pour in dressing, tie securely at top, and tip bag from side to side until dressing is thoroughly distributed.

MORE ABOUT LETTUCE I

If you cut lettuce with a knife, the edges will turn brown. If you tear lettuce leaves, you will bruise them. Whichever method you use is right (or wrong). The most important thing is not to prepare the greens more than a few hours before you plan to eat them.

MORE ABOUT LETTUCE II

Here's a time-saver. Prepare your salad dressing and pour it into the bottom of the salad bowl. Cover it with transparent wrap and then add the salad greens. Just before serving pull out the transparent wrap and let the greens fall into the dressing. Then toss.

DRY YOUR GREENS

Be sure salad greens are perfectly dry or dressing won't cling to the leaves.

KEEPING RAW VEGETABLES FRESH

To keep raw prepared vegetables fresh until your guests arrive, cover them with a damp paper towel and stash them in the refrigerator.

HOW TO FRY PARSLEY AND KEEP IT GREEN

You will have the crispest and brightest green fried parsley if you remember this secret: heat the deep fat to 375°F., but no higher. Dredge the parsley in flour and fry it for two or three minutes until crisp. Serve as a garnish for fried fish or other fried foods.

"FRESH" WAY TO STORE PARSLEY

Rinse the parsley and shake off the excess water. Then wrap it in several thicknesses of damp paper towels. Store the wrapped parsley in a sealed plastic bag in the refrigerator. Pat it dry using dry paper towels before chopping. It is easier to chop parsley that is bone dry. Wet parsley sticks to the knife.

Here is another way to keep parsley green for one or two weeks. After washing and removing the leaves from the stem, place in a jar with a few ice cubes and one tablespoon of cold water. Cover tightly and keep in the refrigerator (not in the freezer).

USE SCISSORS, THE KINDEST CUT OF ALL (SAFER TOO)

Use kitchen scissors for cutting parsley or removing the seeds and pith from peppers. Try to get out of the habit of always grabbing a knife for cutting when, more often than not, scissors will do.

HOW TO KEEP WATERCRESS FRESH

Put watercress stems in a glass of cold water, making sure that the leaves are above the water level. Store in the refrigerator.

HOW TO GET CRISPER CABBAGE FOR COLESLAW

Shred the cabbage and soak it in iced, salted water for fifteen minutes. To get a deliciously distinctive salty taste use kosher or sea salt in the water. Use less salt in the coleslaw dressing.

STRIPTEASE FOR CABBAGE LEAVES

You will need perfect leaves for making stuffed cabbage. The easiest way to prepare the leaves is to immerse the entire head of cabbage in boiling water and stick a long fork into the cabbage. Leave the cabbage in the water for three or four minutes until the leaves have softened and wilted slightly. Then strip the head, one leaf at a time. No further blanching is needed.

Lettuce leaves can be prepared in the same way, but keep the head of lettuce in the boiling water for only a minute.

HOW TO KEEP RED CABBAGE RED

To brighten the color of red cabbage, cook the cabbage uncovered and add a little lemon juice or vinegar to the salted water.

BROCCOLI

Broccoli will cook faster if you split the stem ends.

BEETS

Do not cut the stems of beets too close. Leave one inch of stem and keep the root intact or the beets will "bleed" into the cooking water.

BRUSSELS SPROUTS

Cut a cross in the base of each Brussels sprout and it will cook more quickly.

PREVENT COOKING ODORS

Here is a prescription for odor prevention when you're cooking cabbage, Brussels sprouts, or broccoli. Boil the vegetable for a few minutes, then toss out the water and cover with fresh boiling water.

You will not only have less odor but your vegetables will have a brighter, greener color.

HOW TO KEEP FRESH GINGER FRESH

Save empty pimiento jars and wash them thoroughly. Cut leftover fresh ginger root into small pieces and put into the pimiento jar. Add a little dry sherry, cover the jar, and store it in the refrigerator. Fresh ginger root can also be sliced, wrapped in aluminum foil, and frozen. It defrosts very quickly, but must also be used quickly as it tends to become dry if it is stored in the freezer for more than two weeks.

HOW TO GET A HINT OF GINGER

Force paper-thin slices of fresh ginger root through a garlic press to obtain ginger juice and a delicate hint of flavor.

ALL YOU NEED TO KNOW ABOUT CHILIES

Fresh chilies should be soaked in cold water for an hour to lessen their pungency. Remove the membranes and seeds before using.

Rinse dried chilies in cold water, remove the membranes and seeds and then cut into small pieces.Soak them for thirty minutes to soften before using.

Rinse canned chilies in cold water before using.

HOW TO KEEP CAULIFLOWER WHITE

Snow-white cauliflower should be your goal and the way to achieve it is to cook it, uncovered, in about an inch of milk or water. Do not add salt to the water.

DRIED HERBS

Smell herbs and spices to determine their freshness. If they have no aroma throw them out and buy a new supply. If you still are using the same herbs you had eleven years ago, you might as well be adding a pinch of dust from your vacuum cleaner.

"FRESH" HERBS

To keep fresh herbs on hand, first clean and chop and then put them in ice-cube trays. Fill the trays with water and freeze. When you need "fresh" herbs just melt the ice cubes in a strainer. When the ice melts you'll have nice "fresh" herbs.

WHERE TO STORE HERBS

Store dried herbs and spices in a cool, dark place or they will rapidly lose both flavor and color. The absolutely worst place to keep them is on a shelf over the kitchen stove where they get heated and cooled whenever you use the stove.

RID THE HOUSE OF COOKING ODORS

If your house is filled with cooking odors, the solution is to make yourself some hot apple cider. Simmer the apple juice with a cinnamon stick and three or four cloves. You'll have a delicious drink and the fragrance of the bubbling cider will mask the unpleasant odors.

SECRET TO SLICING MUSHROOMS

Use an egg slicer! You will kick yourself for not having thought of this yourself! Put the rounded side of a very fresh mushroom cap facing downwards and slice away. This is a really terrific short cut because it is not only fast but you also get nice even slices.

NO MORE DARK MUSHROOMS

To keep the natural white color of fresh mushrooms, add a little lemon juice to the butter or margarine in the frying pan.

HOW TO KEEP THE MUSH OUT OF A MUSHROOM

Do not soak mushrooms in water. They are anhydrous, and therefore absorb a surprising amount of water very quickly. Mushrooms need only be wiped with a damp cloth. Cook them rapidly over high heat.

ANOTHER WAY TO KEEP MUSHROOMS FIRM

When the instructions on the package say "wash" and you don't want the mushrooms to absorb so much water, put a couple of tablespoons of flour in a bowl of cold water. Wet your hands with the water in the bowl and rub your fingers quickly over the mushrooms. Wipe with a dry paper towel. You will be surprised how the flour keeps the mushrooms from absorbing so much water.

HOW TO COOK TWO PACKAGES OF FROZEN VEGETABLES AT ONE TIME

When you are cooking two packages of frozen vegetables in the same saucepan, do not double the quantity of water called for on the package. You will drown the poor things. Use the same amount of water for one package as for two. And while we're on the subject never, never attempt to cook more than two packages of frozen vegetables in one pot.

SALT FRIED VEGETABLES AFTER COOKING

Do not salt your fried vegetables until you are ready to serve them. Salt draws moisture to the surface and the moisture makes the vegetables soggy. Incidentally, if you put hot fried vegetables on a cold plate, the steam will be trapped and the same thing will happen. Serve fried vegetables on a warm plate. Do not put them in a covered dish. The steam that collects beneath the lid will fall on top of the vegetables, making them soggy.

WHEN MEAT AND VEGETABLES DO NOT MIX

When vegetables are to accompany roast meat, do not cook the vegetables in the same pan. The vegetables release a lot of moisture causing the meat to be steamed rather than roasted. To give the vegetables that nice meat flavor, baste with meat juices.

HOW TO GET THE CANNED TASTE OUT OF CANNED VEGETABLES

Add a little grated onion to your canned vegetables to improve the taste and get rid of the "tinny" flavor.

HOW TO GET THE CANNED TASTE OUT OF CANNED TOMATOES

To improve the taste of canned tomatoes, empty the tomatoes into a bowl and leave them to "breathe" for an hour before using.

HOW TO PEEL A TOMATO QUICKLY

Force the tines of a fork through the stem end of a tomato. Hold the tomato over a gas flame until the tomato skin splits. It will then peel easily.

HOW TO PEEL A LOT OF TOMATOES QUICKLY

Just drop the tomatoes into boiling water for about one minute. Then remove to a bowl of cold water for another minute. The skin of fully ripened tomatoes can then be slipped off easily.

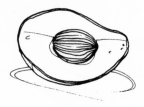

AVOCADOS

Always use a stainless steel knife to cut avocados; carbon steel will cause discoloration.

HOW TO REMOVE THE PIT FROM AN AVOCADO

Here is the secret. Cut the avocado in half, then give the pit a sharp tap with the bottom of a heavy saucepan or the side of a cleaver. It will dislodge easily.

AN OLD SICILIAN SECRET: HOW TO PIT GREEN OLIVES

Give the olive a whack with the bottom of a soup can. The olive splits and the pit pops out.

COLORFUL "BOWL" FOR DIP

Serve your favorite dip in a hollowed red or green pepper, artichoke, or red cabbage. The dip will look marvelous in any one of these vegetables. Remove a thin slice from the bottom of the vegetable so that it will stand upright without tipping.

DECORATING WITH VEGETABLES I

Vegetables make a dynamic centerpiece for the table. To make vegetables such as eggplant, tomatoes, and cucumbers shine, spray them lightly with one of the vegetable-coating sprays. The vegetable coating, which is available at all supermarkets in spray cans, is usually used instead of oil to keep food from sticking to the pan. Give your arrangement a quick spray when it is completed. It will look like a photograph in a glossy magazine.

DECORATING WITH VEGETABLES II

Artichokes make spectacular candle holders. Just cut off the stem so the artichoke will stand straight and not tip to one side. Then remove the center leaves and choke. Lift out the choke and remove only enough leaves to allow the candle to fit securely. If it is difficult to remove the choke with your fingers, use a pair of pliers.

DECORATING WITH VEGETABLES III

Put a champagne glass with a wide bowl in the center of the plate in which you are serving raw vegetables. Fill the glass with a dip for the vegetables. The glass bowl looks dramatic standing high above the vegetables. Use colorful flower blossoms to separate such vegetables as zucchini, mushrooms, broccoli, cauliflower, green beans, cherry tomatoes, and carrots. Depending on the season, your garden, or what is readily available, decorate with azaleas, daisies, statice, chrysanthemum, asters, etc.

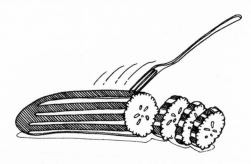

DECORATING WITH VEGETABLES IV

Decorate your salad or other cold food with scalloped cucumbers. Simply leave thin strips of peel when you pare them, score the cucumber lengthwise with the tines of a fork and then slice.

DECORATING WITH VEGETABLES V

Hold individual servings of asparagus together with rings of red pepper. Make the rings more pliable by pouring boiling water over them before using.

DECORATING WITH VEGETABLES VI

Serve black and green olives in a hollowed cucumber. Remove a strip from the base of the cucumber so it will stand without tipping.

HOW TO PREVENT CIRCULAR FOODS
FROM ROLLING

Any round object, whether it is a cantaloupe or grapefuit, can be made to stand securely on a plate by cutting a thin slice from the rounded end.

HULLING STRAWBERRIES

Wash strawberries *before* you hull them or they will lose much of their juice and flavor. Strawberries absorb water very readily, so rinse them as briefly as possible. For the same reason, do not pick strawberries on a rainy day.

FREEZING BERRIES

Place berries—raspberries, strawberries, blackberries, etc.—on a cookie sheet covered with wax paper so that the berries do not touch each other. Place in freezer. When berries are thoroughly frozen, put them into airtight plastic bags and fasten securely.

NO MORE PITH ON YOUR ORANGES

The pith of the orange is the white section beneath the colored orange rind. To remove the pith completely, immerse the whole orange in boiling water before peeling it. The pith will then come away with the rind and there will be no stray pieces clinging to the fruit.

Another easy way to remove the pith when you want to serve sliced oranges is to put the whole fruit in a preheated 350°F. oven for five minutes before peeling them.

MAKING AN ORANGE "APPEELING" TO KIDS

Send a navel orange to school with your child, but make it easy to peel and he'll eat it . . . with no excuses. Here's how. Using a sharp knife, score the peel in eighths. Cut only deep enough so the skin and white pith are broken. Be careful not to jab the juicy orange part.

IMPROVE THE TASTE OF FROZEN ORANGE JUICE

If your family does not enjoy frozen orange juice, make it taste more like fresh by adding the juice of one fresh orange for each small can of concentrate.

HOW TO SAVE A PARTIALLY USED LEMON

When you need only a few drops of lemon juice, do not cut into the lemon. When it is sliced it becomes dry very quickly. Instead, prick it with a fork and squeeze out only the quantity of juice that you need. Seal the lemon skin with butter to exclude the air and return it to the refrigerator.

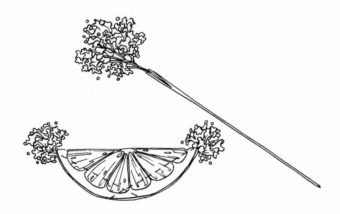

A LEMON THAT WILL NEVER BE A "LEMON"

You can make a lemon garnish look absolutely beautiful. Cut the lemon lengthwise into eight wedges. Next, cut a two-inch slit in a thin bamboo skewer and insert the stem end of a sprig of parsley into it. Push the skewer down into the lemon and out through the rind. Cut off any parsley stem that protrudes. The parsley will stay imbedded in the lemon. Do the same thing at the other end of the wedge.

HOW TO GET MORE JUICE FROM A LEMON

If you heat the lemon slightly before squeezing you will be able to extract considerably more juice. Either immerse the lemon in a bowl of boiling water or put it into a microwave oven for thirty seconds.

HOW TO IMPROVISE A CHERRY PITTER

A large hairpin is almost as effective as a cherry pitter. Insert the rounded end of the hairpin into the cherry at the stem end. Twist the pin and the pit will pop out of the fruit.

FRUIT MOLD MADE EASIER

Layered fruit molds are beautiful but many people shy away from making them. It is time consuming to wait for each layer of fruit to congeal so the fruit will not sink to the bottom. However, if you know which fruits are sinkers and which are floaters, it will be a cinch. Floaters are fresh apple slices, grapefruit segments, pear wedges, strawberries, raspberries, and sliced bananas. Sinkers are fresh grapes, oranges, and almost all canned fruit. Marshmallows and nuts will float. Select some fruit from each category and simply add all the fruit when the gelatin is at the point of setting; the sinkers will sink and the floaters will float.

HOW TO UNMOLD A MOLD

Forget what you've read about unmolding a mold. I say *do not* dip the mold in hot water because all too often the gelatin melts more than you'd like. Instead, run a thin, hot spatula knife around the edge of the mold, rinse a kitchen towel in very hot water, and squeeze the towel as dry as possible. Wrap the hot towel around the mold. It will create just enough heat to enable you to slide the gelatin from its container without any melting.

ANOTHER UNMOLDING SECRET

Wet the serving dish before unmolding your rice or gelatin and you will find it much easier to slide the mold into the center of the plate after it comes out of the form.

WHEN CREAM AND FRUIT DON'T MIX

Cream often curdles when poured over fruit that has acid in it. You can prevent this by adding a pinch of baking soda to the cream. You won't notice any difference in the taste and the baking soda will tame the acid in the fruit.

FROSTED GRAPES

Frosted grapes look spectacular and are easy to make. Dip small bunches or clusters of grapes, one group at a time, into very lightly beaten egg white—that means absolutely no foam. Then dredge in superfine sugar. Spread the grapes on wax paper and put them in the refrigerator to harden the frosting. A few on a plate make an attractive dessert, or they can be served with after-dinner coffee.

HOW TO REMOVE A COCONUT FROM ITS SHELL

Put the whole coconut into a preheated 425°F. oven for ten to fifteen minutes. When you open it, hot or cold, it will be a lot easier to scoop out the meat.

HOW TO PEEL CHESTNUTS WITH EASE

Peeling chestnuts is usually a difficult and tedious job unless you know this secret. Freeze the chestnuts overnight. Then cut an X on the flat side of each of the chestnuts and simmer them for forty minutes. Peel the chestnuts while they are still warm. The shell and brown skin will slip off easily.

HOW TO SEPARATE DATES

When dates stick together, put them in a warm oven for a few minutes and you will not risk tearing the skins when you separate them.

HOW TO "FRESHEN" DRIED FRUIT

When raisins and currants become hard and dry, sprinkle them with a little wine, brandy, lemon juice, or even plain hot water. Put them in the top of a double boiler and heat until they are plump and moist.

ALL YOU NEED TO KNOW ABOUT CUTTING DRIED AND CANDIED FRUIT

Chop or cut candied fruit, raisins, or dates with a knife or scissors dipped (frequently) into a glass of hot water. It makes the job much easier and prevents the fruit from sticking. If the fruit is very sticky, sprinkle it with granulated sugar while chopping.

SOAK PRUNES IN APPLE JUICE

Prunes deserve a better press. They are good, and good for us in more ways than one—and you know the one I mean. Enhance the flavor of prunes by soaking them overnight in apple juice with a slice or two of lemon, or with strong lemon-flavored tea.

ALL YOU NEED TO KNOW ABOUT PINEAPPLE

The best way to discover the ripeness of a pineapple is via the nose test. Smell it. (Pulling the leaf from the crown is an old wives' tale and all you get is a scratched finger from the sharp barbs.) Ripe pineapple should have a very strong pineapple aroma. The top should be green, not dried or shriveled. It should feel firm to the touch, never soft or damp. If the eyes are separated by cracks, the fruit has passed its peak. Do not buy pineapple with a twin green top as it will have twin cores. The best pineapples come by air from Hawaii and are labeled with a picture of an airplane.

HOW TO PEEL A GREEN PLANTAIN

They really should be called plantstain because that's what they do to your hands. To prevent this, peel your plantain under cold running water.

HOW TO COOK FRUIT WITH LESS SUGAR AND GET A SWEET RESULT

Add a little salt even to sweet fruits when poaching them and you wil be surprised how it brings out the sweetness.

A FASTER WAY TO RIPEN FRUIT

When you need to ripen fruit, put it into a brown paper bag, taking care that none of the pieces touch. Then put an apple in the bag. The apple gives off ethylene gas and causes the fruit to ripen rapidly. All fruit, with the exception of bananas, can be ripened in this way.

HOW TO KNOW IF A MELON IS RIPE

Scrape the rind of a watermelon with your fingernail. If it is ripe the green skin will come away easily.

Test a cantaloupe melon with your nose. It should have a sweet, ripe smell. This is a much safer test than feeling the end of a melon. If it smells like melon, it will taste like melon should.

Choose a honeydew melon with a cream-colored skin and fragrant aroma. The nose test is even more important here. The melon will not ripen after it is picked (even if you put it in a bag with an apple!).

HOW TO CUT A MELON BALL SO IT IS ROUND

If your melon balls are flat on one side it is because you are holding the cutter at an angle when you press it into the fruit. Keep the cutter flat on the fruit, press down hard and turn your hand to scoop out the fruit. You'll have a ball!

Watermelon is a good fruit—you eat, you drink and you wash your face.
ENRICO CARUSO

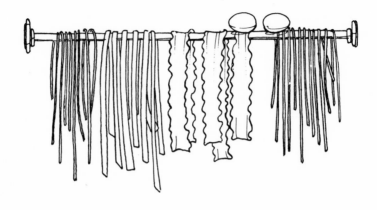

CHAPTER SIX

Rice . . .
Pasta

SECRET FOR FLUFFY RICE I

This is one of the best secrets for making fluffy rice. When the rice is done, remove the lid and cover the pot with two layers of paper toweling. Then cover with a tightly fitting lid and let stand for five, or up to thirty minutes until you are ready to serve it. The excess moisture from the rice will be absorbed by the towels. The end result is light, dry, fluffy rice.

SECRET FOR FLUFFY RICE II

Do not lift the lid or stir the rice as it cooks or the grains will stick together.

SECRET FOR WHITER RICE

Add a teaspon of lemon juice to the water before you cook your rice. Not only will the rice be whiter, the grains will remain separate and not stick together.

HOW TO REHEAT RICE

To reheat rice, spread it in a buttered shallow dish and dot the surface with more butter. Season with salt and pepper and cover the dish with foil. Place in a preheated 350°F oven for fifteen minutes and when you remove it from the oven stir with a fork to fluff it up.

NO-STICK SPAGHETTI

Add a tablespoon of vegetable oil to the boiling water when you cook spaghetti. It prevents the strands from sticking together.

HOW TO COOK PERFECT PASTA

Pasta needs to be cooked in a lot of water. A pound of pasta, sufficient for four people for a main course, should be cooked in a deep pan containing at least five quarts of water, and preferably seven quarts. The water must be boiling furiously before you add a table-spoon of salt and a tablespoon of oil.

Add the pasta immediately after the salt and oil, and keep the water at a steady boil. Stir the pasta occasionally with a pasta rake or wooden fork.

HOW TO DRAIN PASTA

Pasta lovers squabble over the fine points of its preparation as much as baseball fans do when deciding the all-time greatest player. Some insist that a cup of cold water should be added to the boiling pasta in the pot to arrest any further cooking activity. The pasta is then drained through a colander. Others maintain that the pasta should be lifted directly out of the boiling water with a spaghetti rake and placed promptly on the plates.

I don't use either method. I drain the pasta in a colander and let the cold water from the tap run over it for a moment. Why? Because the cold water not only arrests the cooking, it also washes off excess starch. Less starch, less calories. Don't worry that the cold water will cool the pasta; it comes in contact for only a moment, and the internal heat of the pasta is sufficient to combat any external heat loss.

Whichever method you choose, serve the pasta on very hot plates and toss it immediately with the chosen sauce or with butter or oil. Sprinkle it with freshly grated Parmesan cheese, and serve it without a moment's delay.

THE ENERGY-SAVING WAY TO COOK ALMOST PERFECT SPAGHETTI

Purists won't approve of this method, but it works very well. Fill a large pot with water, cover, and heat until the water is boiling briskly. Add salt and one tablespoon of oil. Drop in the spaghetti and let cook until the water is vigorously boiling again. Stir and cover with a lid. Be sure the lid fits snugly. Turn off the heat and let the covered pot stand for twenty minutes. Do not peek until the time is up. So help me, the spaghetti is wonderful. The same technique works for noodles and lasagna: ten minutes for egg noodles—the thin ones—a little longer for the wide noodles. Thirty minutes for lasagna.

NO-STICK DUMPLINGS

You can prevent dumpling batter from sticking to the spoon by dipping the spoon into cold water before you put it into the batter. The batter will slide off the spoon more easily.

LIGHTER DUMPLINGS

You will have perfect dumplings if you steam them for twelve to fifteen minutes without lifting the lid. The problem is how to watch them without lifting the lid. Use a saucepan with a glass lid. Then you can see when they have become light and airy. If you have to lift the lid to check them, steam condenses on the dumplings and they become heavy and leaden.

PANCAKES AHEAD OF TIME

When you will be serving a number of people for breakfast, you may want to make the pancakes ahead of time. The trick is not to stack them one on top of another, because steam causes the pancakes to stick together and become soggy. Instead, line a large roasting pan or baking sheet with cloth or paper towels. Put the pancakes on the towels, arranging them in a single layer. Cover with another towel and continue stacking the pancakes. The pancakes will not be *quite* as good as when they are freshly made, but this is a reasonable compromise and permits you to spend time with your guests.

HOW TO COOK CRÊPES

There are several good recipes for crêpes. Whichever you choose, let the prepared batter rest in the refrigerator for at least an hour—overnight is better. This tenderizes the flour. Be sure the completed batter is thin—like heavy cream. If it is not, add a little more liquid.

For ease and speed of preparation use two frying pans to cook the crêpes. The first should be the size you wish the finished crêpe to be, and the second a little larger. Heat the pans slowly and thoroughly before adding any oil. Pour a little cooking oil into each pan and wipe the pan with a paper towel to take up any excess oil. Don't throw the towel away—you'll need it again. Then, on a medium-low flame, ladle a little batter into the center of the smaller pan and immediately turn the pan from side to side until the bottom of the pan is coated with the least amount of batter possible. If you put too much batter into the pan, pour the excess out. If you didn't put enough into the pan, drizzle a little batter onto any bald spots. After you've done it a couple of times you'll know how much to use. Cook the crêpe until it begins to brown around the edges. Then pick up your crêpe pan and turn it upside down on top of the second pan so that the crêpe drops into this pan to cook on the reverse side. Cook for a minute or less. The reverse side is less brown than the top side. This is a much easier method than using a pancake turner—or trying to flip the crêpe in midair. And two crêpes are cooking at the same time. Using the paper towel with the oil on it, wipe out your pans, and proceed with the next crêpe.

If your pans are not sufficiently hot, the crêpes will not brown properly. If the pan becomes too hot, the crêpe batter may form a clump in the middle of the pan. Wave the pan in the air like a flag to cool it, lower the heat, wipe the surface of the pan with oiled paper towel, and continue cooking the crêpes.

Stir the batter from time to time, as it tends to become thicker at the bottom. If the batter becomes too thick add a little more milk or water until it has thinned to the consistency of heavy cream.

Stack cooked crêpes on a kitchen towel with the unevenly browned side up, so the crêpes will be ready for filling. It is not necessary to separate the crêpes with wax-paper circles. They will not stick together.

TWO GOOD CRÊPE RECIPES

This recipe makes twenty crêpes.
½ cup water
3 eggs
1 cup sifted flour
½ cup milk
salt
2 tablespoons melted butter.

Place all of the ingredients in a blender and blend until smooth. Let rest in refrigerator for an hour or two or overnight before cooking.

This recipe makes eight crêpes.
3 eggs
2 tablespoons flour
1 tablespoon water
1 tablespoon milk
salt

Place all of the ingredients in a blender and blend until smooth. Let rest in refrigerator for an hour or two or overnight before cooking.

HOW TO REHEAT CRÊPES

Butter an oval au gratin or rectangular baking dish and fill it with the stuffed crêpes, arranging them seam side down. Dot the surface of the crêpes with one or two tablespoons of butter. Cover with foil and bake until hot. When covered with a cheese sauce the crêpes should be reheated in the same way, then run under the broiler for three minutes.

No man is lonely while eating
spaghetti—it requires so much attention.
CHRISTOPHER MORLEY

CHAPTER SEVEN

Cakes . . .
    Cookies . . .
        Other Desserts . . .
            Bread

ROUND OR SQUARE CAKES?

If you have a choice, bake cakes in round pans rather than in square pans. Cake corners in square pans tend to cook first and cakes may become unevenly cooked or even burn.

GLASS BAKING PANS

When baking in a pan made of glass, the oven temperature should be reduced by 25°F.

FINGERS ARE BETTER

When greasing a cake or baking pan, use your fingers. They work with far greater efficiency than any other device. This may seem obvious, but many people use butter wrappers, wax paper, or paper towels. The only method that comes close to fingers is to spread the butter around the pan with a piece of soft bread. Then use the bread for croutons.

CAKE-PAN DUSTER

When the recipe calls for dusting your cake tin with flour, use a big bath powder puff and you will have the best duster you can imagine.

KEEPING FLOUR INSECT FREE

There are two ways you can outsmart the weevils, those insidious little black insects that appear like magic in flour or grain bags. Put a bay leaf in each package. Another way to outsmart the little devils is to put all grain and flour packages in the refrigerator.

WHEN TO REMOVE CAKE FROM PAN

Let a baked cake stand for five minutes—no longer—in the cake pan, then unmold it onto a wire cake-cooling rack. The rack permits air to circulate freely beneath the cake. If the cake is put on top of the counter, the trapped steam will make the underside of the cake soggy.

HOW TO RETRIEVE A LIGHTLY BURNED CAKE

Rather than using a knife to scrape off burned cake crumbs, use a coarse grater and grate away the scorched edges carefully.

BE YOUR OWN CAKE DOCTOR I

If a cake bakes unevenly, the cake pan may have been placed too close to the side of the oven. The oven wall creates a secondary source of heat. If the bottom and sides of the cake burn, the cake may have been placed on too high a rack or two cake pans may have been placed too close to each other. The metal pans create a secondary source of reflected heat.

BE YOUR OWN CAKE DOCTOR II

When the surface of the cake cracks (other than pound cakes, in which this always happens), either too much flour was used or the oven temperature was too high.

BE YOUR OWN CAKE DOCTOR III

If the cake has a soggy bottom, it may have been left in the cake pan too long after baking. Unmold the cake onto a wire cake-cooling rack five minutes after removing from the oven.

BE YOUR OWN CAKE DOCTOR IV

If the cake is too dry, an insufficient amount of butter, oil, or sugar may have been used.

BE YOUR OWN CAKE DOCTOR V

If a cake sinks in the middle, either it was not baked long enough or it contained too much butter or sugar. Test the center of the cake with a toothpick. If it comes out clean and the sides of the cake have begun to shrink from the pan, remove it from the oven.

BE YOUR OWN CAKE DOCTOR VI

If the cake batter flows over the sides of the cake pan, it either contained too much butter, or the pan was too full. Allow at least one-half-inch for the batter to rise.

HOW TO PREVENT A CHEESECAKE FROM SINKING IN THE MIDDLE

To prevent cheesecake from sinking in the middle, beat three tablespoons of flour into the cheese mixture before baking.

HOT TIP FOR A COOLING CAKE

Spray the wire rack with vegetable coating spray (sold in the supermarkets to prevent food from sticking to pans) and the cake will not stick.

SWEET IDEA TO KEEP CAKE FROM STICKING

Sprinkle a little powdered sugar in the center of your empty cake platter in a diameter a little smaller than the cake. The cake won't stick to the plate.

HOW TO MATCH CAKE LAYERS

Before you slice a cake in half, cut a vertical dressmaker's notch in the side. Split and fill the cake and realign the sides using the notch as a guide.

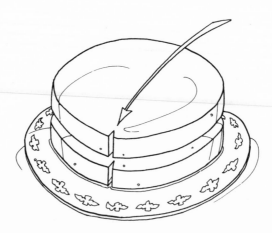

HOW TO HAVE A CLEAN CAKE PLATTER

To protect the cake platter from spills while you are frosting a cake, slip strips of wax paper beneath the edge of the cake. Any spills will fall onto the paper instead of the plate. Remove the paper carefully.

HOW TO SPLIT A CAKE EVENLY I

It is all too easy to slice a cake so you end up with one side of the layer thicker than the other. To avoid this insert toothpicks half way up the side of the cake making a circle of toothpicks. Insert the knife above the toothpicks and they will form a guide for a perfectly even slice. Use a knife with a serrated edge to cut the cake.

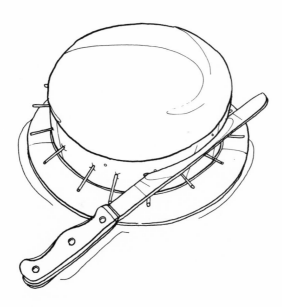

HOW TO SPLIT A CAKE EVENLY II

Another way to cut a cake evenly. Again, use the toothpicks as a guide but cut the cake with a long piece of strong button thread. Cross the ends of the thread as you pull it toward you through the cake.

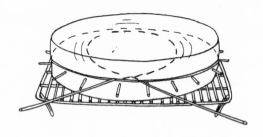

A PERFECT FIT

If you are concerned that cake layers spread with whipped cream may slide away from each other enroute to the table, secure them in place using thin bamboo skewers. Make sure you leave part of the skewer showing above the surface of the cake so you can find them again.

HOW TO KEEP A MOIST CAKE MOIST

To prevent a partially eaten cake from becoming dry, slip an apple or lemon alongside the exposed sides of the cut wedge. Cover the cake with a cake cover or transparent wrap. If the cake is frosted, insert several toothpicks into the frosting so the wrap will not touch the frosting and "tear" when it is lifted off.

HOW TO RETRIEVE BOILED ICING

If your boiled icing turns into a hard mass of sugar, just add a few drops of white or cider vinegar. It will help enormously and, strangely enough, you will not be able to taste the vinegar.

HOW TO MELT CHOCOLATE WITHOUT USING A DISH

Keep the chocolate in its original wrapper and then set it on a piece of folded foil. Put it into a preheated 300°F oven for ten minutes until it has melted. Scrape the chocolate from the paper and you will not have a dish to wash.

HOW TO SPREAD FROSTING ON A CRUMBLY CAKE

To avoid having cake crumbs in the frosting, brush the surface and sides of the cake with warm, strained apricot preserves and then freeze the cake until it is firm. Then frost the cake. There will be a slight flavor of apricot, which is very pleasant.

HOW TO KEEP CAKE FROSTING MOIST

To prevent frosting from becoming dry and cracked, add half a teaspoon of baking powder to each cup of powdered sugar called for in the recipe.

KEEP ICING IN ITS PLACE

Add a tablespoon of sifted flour or cornstarch to each cup of sifted confectioners' sugar. The icing will remain thin but will have sufficient body so that it will not slide from the cake.

CAKE-DECORATING TRICK

Short pieces of macaroni pushed into a frosted party cake can be used to hold tiny flowers or candles.

INSTANT FROSTING

Here's how to make frosted cupcakes with a minimum of fuss. Place a small piece of chocolate from a candy bar on top of each cupcake as soon as it comes out of the oven. Cover each cupcake with foil. Wait until the chocolate has melted and then spread it evenly over the cupcake, using a metal spatula that has been dipped in cold water.

CANDY IS DANDY, BUT NOT ON A CANDY THERMOMETER

When you are making candy or preparing sugar syrup, keep a tall glass of hot water next to the stove. Dunk the candy thermometer into the water after you test the syrup. This will prevent the sugar from hardening and clinging to the thermometer.

SUGAR SYRUP SECRETS

Scrupulous cleanliness is essential when you are making a sugar syrup. The pan must be washed and dried carefully just before it is used as even the tiniest trace of grease will spoil the syrup. Do not stir the syrup after the sugar has dissolved. Wash down any sugar crystals from the side of the pan with a pastry brush that has been dipped into a glass of warm water.

FAST AS MOLASSES

Rinse your glass measuring cup in cold water before adding corn syrup, molasses, liquid, honey or any other sticky substance. The syrup can be poured quickly from the measuring cup and the cup will be easier to wash.

STABILIZE WHIPPED CREAM I

Whipped cream usually becomes liquid at the bottom of the bowl during the interval before serving. To correct this, put the whipped cream into a strainer lined either with a paper towel or cheesecloth. The liquid will drain out while the whipped cream is waiting to be put to use.

STABILIZE WHIPPED CREAM II

Another tip to keep whipped cream "together." Beat the white of one egg with each pint of cream.

STABILIZE WHIPPED CREAM III

And yet another. Add one tablespoon instant vanilla pudding while whipping. The cream will have a firmer texture and won't become liquid at the bottom of the bowl so easily.

STABILIZE WHIPPED CREAM IV

A final secret. Add a pinch of unflavored gelatin before whipping.

A PINCH IN THE RIGHT PLACE

Did you know that a pinch of salt added to heavy cream will enable it to be beaten faster?

HOW TO FREEZE WHIPPED CREAM

Did you know you can freeze whipped cream? Just beat the cream until it is firm and drop it by spoonfuls onto a cookie sheet lined with foil. Freeze the cream, then take it from the freezer and carefully wrap each cream ball in a transparent wrap. Overwrap in freezer wrap or put into a container such as an egg carton. Take the cream from the freezer as you need it. It defrosts very quickly. Next time you whip cream, whip an extra batch and freeze it. Whipping cream doubles in volume. One cup makes two cups of whipped cream.

WHIPPED TOPPING WITHOUT CREAM

Here's a tip if you don't have cream and you need whipped cream to complete a dessert. Mix a thoroughly mashed banana with an egg white. Then beat with an electric beater, adding plenty of sugar and vanilla to taste. Whip until topping stands in peaks.

HOW TO WHIP EVAPORATED MILK—SUCCESSFULLY

Pour chilled evaporated milk onto a cookie sheet with one-half-inch sides. Put the cookie sheet into the freezer until small particles of ice have formed. Meantime, chill the mixing bowl and beaters. Pour the chilled milk into the chilled bowl and beat until the whipped milk is of the correct consistency. Chilling is the secret of success.

ALL YOU NEED TO KNOW ABOUT MERINGUE

Do not attempt to cook a meringue on a wet or humid day. It will absorb the moisture from the air and become soft and sticky.

To prevent a crisp-baked meringue from sticking to the baking pan, cook it on a cookie sheet lined with parchment paper. In preparing the meringue mixture add one-quarter cup of sugar for each egg white.

HOW TO CUT CRISP MERINGUE

Cut crisp baked meringue into serving pieces using a knife dipped in cold water.

ORANGE AND LEMON RIND

To remove orange and lemon rind from the grater, bang the grater on the counter or brush the rind from the grater with a dry pastry brush.

NUTTY SECRETS

When chopping nuts in a blender or food processor, add a tablespoon of flour for each cup of nuts to keep them from forming clumps.

Toasted nuts have a better flavor when baked into cakes. Spread the ground nuts on a flat pan and put them in a preheated 350 °F. oven for eight to ten minutes until they are lightly browned. Stir with a fork to distribute the heat evenly.

NUTS TO THE FREEZER

Opened cans of nuts will stay much fresher if kept in the freezer. If the nuts come in bags, put the bag into a plastic tub (the kind margarine or cottage cheese comes in) before freezing.

WHOLE WALNUTS—NOT PIECES

To get a whole nut from its shell, stand the nut on *end* and tap the top of the shell gently with a small hammer. Do not hit the nut on its side. The shell will fall away and the nut will be easy to get out.

HOW TO SEPARATE THE NUT FROM THE SHELL

When shelling a large quantity of nuts, some shells may become mixed with the nutmeat. To separate the pieces of shell put the nuts in a bowl of water. The nuts will sink and the shells will float to the surface and can easily be lifted from the water. Place nuts on a paper towel until thoroughly dry.

MORE ABOUT NUTS

To prevent nuts from sinking to the bottom of a cake, toss them lightly in flour before adding them to the cake batter.

ANOTHER VERSION OF THE OLD SHELL GAME

To remove pecans from their shells with ease, cover them with boiling water and let them stand until the water is cold. Then tap the end with a hammer.

QUICK TEST FOR BAKING POWDER

If you are a sometime baker and the baking powder has been on your shelf longer than you care to admit, it is wise to test it before using. Mix a teaspoon of baking powder in half a cup of hot water. If it bubbles furiously, it is still active and can safely be used.

HOW TO MAKE BAKING POWDER . . . OR ALMOST

Nothing is more infuriating, when you feel like baking, to find that you have no baking powder and no neighbor to borrow from. Here's a secret for a very adequate substitute. For every cup of flour in your recipe, use two teaspoons cream of tartar, one teaspoon baking soda, and one-half teaspoon salt as a substitute.

GETTING THE LID OFF THE CAN

If you have difficulty removing the small recessed lid from a can of baking powder, roll it underfoot for a few seconds and then try again.

SWEET IDEA WHEN MAKING COOKIES

Use powdered sugar instead of flour when you're rolling cookies. The dough gets a bit sweeter, but will not toughen as it often does when you use extra flour for rolling.

HOW TO MANAGE CRUMBLY COOKIE DOUGH

Do not add more liquid to crumbly cookie dough. Instead leave the dough at room temperature for about an hour until it has softened. It will then be easier to roll.

HOW TO DEAL WITH A HARD COOKIE

When cookies become too hard, put them in an airtight tin with a slice of fresh bread. The cookies will absorb the moisture from the bread and soften very slightly. Another method of softening cookies is to wet a paper towel and lay it on a piece of aluminum foil. Put both foil and towel in the tin on top of the cookies with the paper towel uppermost.

HOW TO MAKE MARVELOUS OATMEAL COOKIES

Toast the oatmeal *before* baking it into cookies. Spread the oatmeal on a cookie sheet and bake it in a preheated 300°F. for eight to ten minutes until it has colored lightly. Cool the oatmeal before folding it into the other ingredients.

FANTASTIC GINGERBREAD SECRET

Try using coffee instead of water in your batter. The result is superb.

THE COLD FACT

Bake cookies on cool cookie sheets or the batter will spread too quickly.

COOL IDEA FOR HOT COOKIE SHEETS

When you are making several batches of cookies and you do not want to wait for the cookie sheets to cool before baking the next batch, this is what you do. Simply run cold water on the *underside* of the cookie sheet and you will find it cools very quickly. Just make sure you do not get any water on the top surface of the sheet or you will have to wash it.

COOKIE CONTAINERS

Save coffee cans or shortening cans. Use them to store cookies. Cover with contact paper for a more attractive effect. Store cookies in containers with tightly fitting lids and do not mix crisp and soft cookies or they will all become soft.

HOW TO MAKE FLAKIER PASTRY

Keep your fat cold. And hard. No matter whether you use butter, margarine, lard, or shortening, the fat should be very cold before it is blended into the flour.

IF YOU DO NOT HAVE A ROLLING PIN

If you do not have a rolling pin, use a round, tightly capped bottle filled with ice water.

NO-STICK ROLLING PIN

Pastry dough will not stick to your rolling pin if you put the dough in the freezer or refrigerator until it is well chilled. In this way you can avoid having to use any additional flour. Too much flour toughens the pastry.

HOW TO USE A PASTRY BRUSH

Always wet a pastry brush in cold water. Squeeze out the excess water from the bristles before each use, to make it flexible. A new paint brush makes a good substitute for a pastry brush.

HOW TO FILL A PASTRY BAG

If you have difficulty filling a pastry bag, drop the tip into a wide-mouthed jar or bottle and drape the sides over the edges of the jar. You will then have both hands free to scrape the mixture into the pastry bag. Do not fill the bag more than three-quarters full or it will erupt from the wrong end. Twist the top of the filled pastry bag to prevent the mixture from emerging from the wrong end. Use the heel of your hand to squeeze the mixture through the nozzle. Direct the nozzle or tip with the other hand.

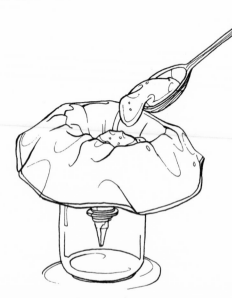

HOW TO PROTECT CREAM PUFFS

Rinse your cookie sheet with cold water after you grease it. The droplets on the pan will prevent your cream puffs from having scorched bottoms.

HOW TO AVOID A SOGGY PASTRY BOTTOM I

Sprinkle a little cornmeal in the pie plate before fitting in the crust. The cornmeal will absorb any excess liquid from the pie filling.

HOW TO AVOID A SOGGY PASTRY BOTTOM II

Another way to keep that bottom crust crisp is to brush a little beaten egg over the crust just before baking. It prevents the juice from being absorbed by the pastry.

HOW TO SOFTEN A HARD MARSHMALLOW

When marshmallows become dry and hard, put a piece of soft, fresh bread in the package and, in a day or two, the marshmallows will freshen by themselves.

WHAT TO DO IF YOUR HONEY HAS HARDENED

If your honey crystallizes, put the uncovered jar in a saucepan of hot water and heat over a low flame until it is smooth again. The jar could also be put in a gas oven overnight; the heat of the pilot light will soften it.

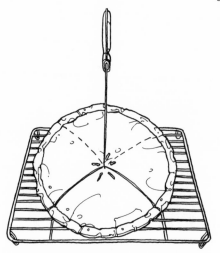

HOW TO CUT A PIE INTO FIVE EVEN PIECES

It is simple to cut a pie into four pieces. It is even easy to cut it into six pieces. But have you ever tried to cut it into five pieces? Five *even* pieces. You can. Cut a Y into the pie, then cut the two larger sections in half.

NO-STICK HARD CANDY

Unwrapped hard candies will not stick together if you sprinkle them with a little granulated sugar before packing them into a container. Always select a container with a tightly fitting lid to exclude the air.

NO MORE SPILLED CANDY

When you are making candy, you can prevent the mixture from boiling over by buttering the upper third of the saucepan.

"GLUE" YOUR LADY FINGERS

When you want to put ladyfingers around the edge of a mold and you want them to stay put, "glue" them to the sides with butter. It really works.

HOW TO "SKIN" A PUDDING

Keep a skin from forming on top of a pudding or custard by covering it with a piece of transparent wrap. The wrap must touch the surface of the pudding to make it airtight. Remove the covering just before serving.

PERFECT BAKED CUSTARD

Do not beat the eggs before adding the milk. The eggs and milk should only be stirred until they are combined. Overbeating makes the custard sink in the middle. Always bake custard in a water bath. Put the custard cups in a large container and add sufficient hot, not boiling water to a point halfway up the sides of the cups. Bake the custard until it is barely set. It will become firmer as it cools. Do not overbake or holes will appear and the custard will not have a delicate consistency. Chill baked custard for four hours before unmolding.

HOW TO TURN EMPTY ORANGE SHELLS INTO SERVING DISHES

After you have squeezed orange juice, save your empty orange shells. Scoop out the membranes using a pointed teaspoon and then freeze them until you are ready to fill them with ice cream or chocolate mousse. Don't cut "teeth" around edge; as the orange rind freezes, the "teeth" are inclined to become misshapen. Decorate with a few nuts or coconut.

Here's the recipe I use to fill the shell:

1 quart vanilla ice cream, softened
1 small can orange-juice concen-
    trate, thawed
¼ cup Grand Marnier
¼ cup toasted almonds, chopped

Stir all ingredients together until thoroughly mixed. Pour into prepared orange shells. Freeze.

GELATIN

All foods prepared with gelatin are best eaten the day they are made, or they become rubbery. Do not boil unflavored gelatin. When it cools, it will form strings and lose some of its setting qualities. Heat it only until a clear liquid has formed.

HOW TO KEEP THE ICE OUT OF HOMEMADE ICE CREAM

If you wrap your ice-cream container very tightly in aluminum foil you will prevent ice crystals from forming when you freeze it.

EVEN BETTER COFFEE ICE CREAM

If you like coffee ice cream, sprinkle a little instant coffee granules on top of it. It looks beautiful and tastes even better.

GETTING A RISE OUT OF YOUR DOUGH

As you know, bread dough must rise in a warm spot. Try putting it on top of your refrigerator. You'll be surprised to find how warm this spot is. Another good warm place is inside the unlit gas oven. The heat of the pilot light provides the ideal environment for yeast dough. If you do not have a gas oven, stand the bowl of dough on your kitchen counter on a warm heating pad. Take care not to let the dough rise to more than double the original size.

HOW TO GET A SHINY CRUST

To get a shiny crust on homemade bread, brush it with a touch of white vinegar a few minutes before it is fully baked. Return it to the oven until baking is completed.

GREAT GARLIC BREAD

Garlic bread will have a better flavor and leave sweeter breath if the garlic cloves are first boiled in water for three or four minutes. Then crush the garlic and combine it with oil or butter.

FREEZE BREAD

Store bread in the freezer. It will not go stale and will defrost almost instantly if it was presliced.

HOW TO REVIVE STALE BREAD

Italian and French breads became stale quickly. To revive them, put the slices of bread into a dampened brown paper bag and then bake in a preheated 350°F. oven for ten minutes. Stale loaves and rolls can also be revived. Spray them lightly with cold water before putting them into a *dry* paper bag. The bag is then put into a 375°F. oven for seven minutes.

SALT BOXES FOR BREAD CRUMBS

Make double use of your salt boxes. When all the salt has been used up, store your homemade bread crumbs in the boxes.

NO MORE SOGGY SANDWICHES

Tuna fish and other moist fillings tend to cause soggy sandwiches. To protect the bread, spread it generously with butter or margarine.

SLICE YOUR CALORIES IN HALF

If you slice your sliced bread in half, horizontally, you will have only half the calories. To slice paper-thin bread, first freeze thin-sliced bread until it is firm enough to cut easily. Or you can freeze an unsliced loaf of bread until it is firm, but not solid. Then slice as thin as you wish. This method is not only great for those watching their weight, but is also good for making melba toast and dainty tea sandwiches.

INSTANT SOFT BUTTER

Here are several secrets for when the recipe calls for soft butter. You can grate the butter. You can also soften it in a bowl of warm water or put the butter in a warm bowl and cover it with another warm bowl.

HOW TO HAVE THE PRETTIEST BISCUITS ON YOUR BLOCK

Your biscuits, pancakes, or waffles will turn a beautiful and mouth-watering brown color if you add a teaspoon of sugar to the batter. That's not enough to change the taste, but, oh, what wonders it will do for the color.

HOLD THAT CAN

Empty cans have many uses. Save fruit or vegetable cans to use as gelatin molds. When the gelatin has set, open the bottom of the can with a can opener and slide out the mold. Empty coffee cans can be used for baking bread and empty tuna cans are great molds for baking bagels.

The less one eats, the more he eats
I meane he liveth longer to eat more.
STEFANO GAAZZO, 1574

CHAPTER EIGHT

*Miscellaneous . . . Frozen Foods
. . . Outdoor Cooking . . .
Beverages . . . Pots and Pans
. . . Serving a Crowd . . .
Ingredient Instructions . . .
Metric Conversion*

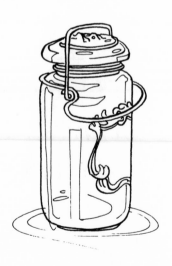

THE JOYS OF A FAT CAN

Save all your bacon fat and use it for future cooking. To obtain clear fat, pour the cooled fat into a can containing an inch or two of cold water. Burned bacon bits will sink to the bottom and the pure fat will rise to the surface and harden. Store the fat in the refrigerator.

A FAST BOUQUET GARNI

Use a metal teaball for holding garlic, herbs, and spices. It is less trouble than tying them into a cheesecloth bag.

OLIVE OIL SECRET

To prevent olive oil from becoming rancid, add two small lumps of sugar to each quart as soon as opened. This is so little sugar that the taste of the olive oil is not affected.

HOW TO CHECK THE WATER LEVEL IN A DOUBLE BOILER

When cooking in a double boiler it is important to be sure the water in the lower pot has not boiled away. If you put some marbles or pebbles in the pot they will rattle when the water level becomes dangerously low.

NO-STICK TONGS

Dip tongs in the hot fat before lifting out fried food to prevent the food from sticking to the tongs.

HOW TO COPE WITH A FAT FIRE ON TOP OF THE STOVE

If possible, cover the pan with a lid to exclude the air; smother the flames with baking soda, or a large quantity of flour. Do not attempt to put out the fire with water or try to carry the flaming pan to the sink. You will very likely drop it as the flames roar over your hands. If you are not absolutely sure you can handle the fire quickly, do not hesitate to call the fire department for help.

NO-ODOR FRYING

Put a tablespoon of vinegar into the cold fat to be used for deep frying. It will reduce the cooking odor.

DEFROSTING SECRET FOR BREADED FOOD

Frozen food that is to be breaded must be completely defrosted and thoroughly dried with paper towels. Then dredge in flour, bread-crumbs, or batter, and food will not spatter, the coating will not fall off, and the cooking fat will not become waterlogged.

STORING FROZEN CASSEROLES

Freeze food in the casserole in which you plan to serve it. Line the casserole with heavy-duty foil. Add the food and when it is solidly frozen, remove it from the container and wrap it in freezer wrap. Remove the foil and reheat it in its original casserole when you are ready to serve.

FREEZING SECRET

When you are freezing food, remember that cold travels downwards and heat rises. So, if you want to freeze food quickly, cover it with another food that is solidly frozen.

FREEZING MORE POP IN YOUR POPCORN

Try freezing popcorn kernels and pop them while they are still frozen. They will pop better and more completely.

FREE FREEZING CONTAINERS

Save plastic tubs (the kind margarine or cottage cheese comes in) for odds and ends in the freezer. The smaller the container, the faster the food will freeze. Don't use ordinary glass jars; freezing makes them brittle.

HOW TO SPEED UP THE KETCHUP

A new bottle of ketchup will pour easily if you insert a drinking straw into the bottle. Push it all the way to the bottom of the jar and stir the contents. Then pour.

HOW TO MAKE SALT STICK TO NUTS

The trick is to use egg white instead of oil, butter, or margarine. Toss the nuts in a bowl containing an egg white. Then spread the nuts on a cookie sheet, sprinkle them with coarse salt, and roast them in a preheated 300°F. oven until golden. The egg whites hold the salt without a hint of grease.

MAKE YOUR OWN SUPERFINE SUGAR

When you need superfine sugar and all you have is granulated sugar, put it in a blender or food processor and presto, you will have superfine sugar.

SALT AND SWEET BUTTER

Foods cooked in salted butter take on a richer shade of golden brown color than those cooked in unsalted butter. The salt, sodium chloride, caramelizes to color the food.

NO-BURN BUTTER

You know how easily butter burns when you use it for frying? To minimize the danger of burning add one tablespoon of peanut oil for every two tablespooons of butter.

NO MORE DRIPPING CREAM PITCHER

Rub the spout of a cream pitcher with softened butter and you will eliminate drips.

HOW TO CUT MARSHMALLOWS

Dip your scissors or knife into a glass of cold water every few seconds and you will be able to cut marshmallows with amazing speed.

EASY WAY TO FIND THE SIZE OF A MOLD

When you don't know the size of your mold, fill the mold with water and then pour the water into a measuring cup. All you need to know is that four cups equal one quart.

HOW TO DRY HERBS

To shorten the procedure and obtain a dry leaf, hose your garden herbs the day before you plan to pick and dry them. Line a cookie sheet with a double thickness of paper towels. Scatter the herbs on the towels and dry them in the sun or leave them in a gas oven with only the pilot light on for four hours.

HAND-Y TEST FOR TESTING THE OUTDOOR GRILL

Use your hand! Hold your hand over the grill at the level at which the food will be cooked. If you can leave it there for a slow count of eight, your fire is low. A count of five indicates a medium and three is a hot fire.

COOKING ON A SPIT

Allow an additional thirty minutes' cooking time for meats cooked on a spit as compared with oven roasting.

COOL YOUR BARBECUE FIRE

Use a whisk broom to sprinkle enough water onto a barbecue fire to cool it down without extinguishing it.

DOUSING FLAMES

When your barbecue fire flares up because of fat drippings, lay a lettuce leaf over the flame. The flame subsides and the lettuce disintegrates.

EASIER BARBECUE CLEANUP

Rub the bottom of saucepans used on the outdoor grill with soap or detergent. The dirt will rinse away without any problems.

COFFEE FOR THE GANG

To make twenty cups of coffee, you will need one-half pound of regular coffee and four quarts of water.

FREEZE COFFEE

To preserve the flavor, store ground coffee in the freezer.

SWEETENING THE POT

To keep the coffee pot clean and sweet, fill it with water and add a tablespoon or two of baking soda. Simmer very gently for an hour and rinse carefully before reusing.

MAKE INSTANT COFFEE TASTE LIKE FRESH BREWED

Boil instant coffee for about thirty seconds, then turn off the heat and let stand for a minute before serving. This easy tip makes quite a difference.

WHAT TO DO WHEN YOU RUN OUT OF COFFEE FILTERS

Try facial tissues. They work almost as well.

COOL IDEA FOR ICED TEA AND COFFEE

Don't dilute your iced tea or coffee by using ordinary ice cubes. Make the ice cubes from tea or coffee, and you'll get a drink with more flavor—the way it was meant to taste.

SUGAR CUBES WITH A DIFFERENCE

For tea with a delicious difference use sugar cubes that have been rubbed over the surface of an orange rind. The sugar picks up the aromatic oils from the fruit.

SWEET SECRET: LESS SUGAR

You will need less sugar in iced tea if you add the sugar while the tea is still hot.

HOW TO MAKE LUMP-FREE COCOA

You will find it a lot easier to make smooth cocoa if you mix the powder with sugar and a little cold milk before adding the remaining milk, heated.

"SKIN" YOUR COCOA

To prevent a skin forming on the cocoa, whip it with a tiny wire whisk or stir it rapidly with a fork.

HOW TO PREVENT SCORCHED MILK

Rinse the saucepan in cold water and do not dry it before adding the milk. This will minimize the danger of scorching. Heat the milk over a low flame.

CHINESE SECRET FOR HOT TOWELS

It is always a delight to eat in a Chinese or Japanese restaurant and be offered hot towels before eating or between courses. You too can charm your guests with this Oriental custom by dampening towels and wrapping them in foil. Put the towels in a hot oven for a few minutes. Hot towels are a very welcome freshener after eating fried chicken, ribs, or butter-drenched lobster.

CHOPSTICKS SAVVY

When eating with chopsticks, imagine you are picking up a delicate butterfly. This will prevent you from gripping the sticks so anxiously that they cross.

WARM PLATES FOR A CROWD . . . EASILY

Put the plates in your dishwasher and turn the dial to the drying cycle. Your plates will be piping hot.

LEFTOVERS

If you are planning to have leftovers from a roast, slice the meat from both ends leaving the rarer center for other uses.

Cooked foods should be wrapped and chilled as soon as possible after it becomes apparent that there are indeed leftovers. A roast that sits exposed to the air for several hours and cheeses that have sweated out their butterfat while you entertained your guests so charmingly in another room can never be restored to their former greatness.

Add mustard, horseradish, herbs, spices, lemon juice, or a freshly cooked vegetable to leftovers to brighten the taste of the food.

It is better to add various leftovers to several new dishes rather than to empty the refrigerator in one gigantic sweep, dumping all into a casserole or calling it "Chinese food."

KEEPING OLIVES FRESH

Store leftover olives in oil. They'll keep perfectly, and you can always reuse the oil.

HOW TO MAKE AN ODD-SHAPED LID

To make a lid for an oval or oddly shaped pan, heat the pan on top of the stove until it is hot. Cover the pan with a piece of wax paper. Press the paper onto the top rim of the pan and an outline of the pan will form on the paper. Use a pair of scissors to cut out the outline. Drop the wax-paper "lid" into the pan so it is touching the food. The paper will not burn.

HOW TO SEASON AN IRON PAN, A CRÊPE PAN, AND AN OMELET PAN

Half fill the pan with peanut or vegetable oil. Heat until tiny bubbles appear in the oil. Remove the pan from the heat and leave it to stand for twelve hours. Tip out the oil (it can be reused). The pan should never again be washed. Wipe it with paper towels after each use. If there is a particle of food sticking to the pan, rub it away using a little salt as an abrasive.

SERVING A CROWD

Quantities to Serve 100 People

Useful block parties; PTA get-togethers; family reunions; Fourth of July outings; fund-raising parties.

MEAT		DESSERTS	
Hamburger	35 lbs.	Ice cream	5 gals.
Beef	40 lbs.	Cakes	8
Roast pork	40 lbs.	Pies	17
Ham	40 lbs.	Fruit cocktail	3 gals.
Frankfurters	25 lbs.		
Chicken	50 lbs.		

VEGETABLES		BEVERAGES	
		Milk	5 gals.
		Tomato juice	4 gals.
Potatoes	35 lbs.	Coffee	3 lbs.
Baked beans	5 gals.	Sugar	3 lbs.
Cabbage (slaw)	20 lbs.	Cream	3 qts.
Carrots	30 lbs.		
Potato salad	12 qts.		
Lettuce	20 heads		

INTERPRETING INGREDIENT INSTRUCTIONS

How Much is a Dash?

Few grains	less than ⅛ teaspoon
Pinch	less than ¼ teaspoon
Dash	not more than ¼ teaspoon
Size of walnut	1 round tablespoon
Size of egg	¼ cup
Heaping cupful	1 cup leveled plus 3 or 4 tablespoons
Scant cup	1 cup leveled, then 2 tablespoons removed
One wine glass	½ cup
3 teaspoons	1 tablespoon
2 tablespoons	1 ounce or ⅛ cup
4 tablespoons	¼ cup
5 tablespoons + 1 teaspoon	⅓ cup
8 tablespoons	½ cup
Juice of 1 lemon	3–4 tablespoons
Juice of 1 orange	¼–½ cup

OVEN TEMPERATURES	DEGREES FAHRENHEIT
Very slow oven	250–275
Slow oven	300–325
Moderate oven	350–375
Quick or hot oven	400–425
Very hot oven	450–475
Extremely hot oven	500–525

METRIC CONVERSION MADE EASY

	when you know	*you can find*	*if you multiply by*
WEIGHT			
(mass)	ounces	grams	28
	pounds	kilograms	0.45
	teaspoons	millileters	5
LIQUID	tablespoons	millileters	15
VOLUME	ounces	milliliters	30
	pints	liters	0.47
	quarts	liters	0.95
	gallons	liters	3.8
TEMPERATURE	degrees Fahrenheit	degrees Celsius	5/9ths after subtracting 32

Metric weights and measures go up (and down) by tens.

Some examples:

Kilo means a thousand. A kilometer is a thousand meters;
Centi means a hundredth. A centimeter is a hundredth of a meter;
Milli means a thousandth. A millimeter is a thousandth of a meter

Metric abbreviations:

kilogram	kg
liter	1
milliliter	ml
gram	g
centimeter	cm

For Metric Recipes:

When you know	Multiply by	To find
millileters	0.2	teaspoons
millileters	0.6	tablespoons
millileters	0.03	fluid ounces
millileters	0.004	cups
liters	0.42	cups
liters	2.11	pints
liters	1.06	quarts
liters	0.26	gallons

Oven Temperatures:

FAHRENHEIT DEGREES	CELSIUS DEGREES
200 °F.	93 °C.
350 °F.	177 °C.
400 °F.	204 °C.
450 °F.	232 °C.
500 °F.	260 °C.

The intention of every other piece of prose may be discussed and even mistrusted; but the purpose of a cookery book is one and unmistakable. Its object can conceivably be no other than to increase the happiness of mankind.

JOSEPH CONRAD

INDEX OF SECRETS

(in order of appearance in the book)

CHAPTER ONE   EGGS . . . CHEESE . . . APPETIZERS

CHAPTER TWO   SAUCE . . . SOUP

CHAPTER THREE   MEAT . . . POULTRY

CHAPTER FOUR   FISH . . . SHELLFISH

CHAPTER FIVE   VEGETABLES . . . FRUIT

CHAPTER SIX   RICE . . . PASTA

CHAPTER SEVEN CAKES . . . COOKIES . . .
OTHER DESSERTS . . . BREAD

CHAPTER EIGHT   MISCELLANEOUS

INDEX

YOUR PERSONAL SECRETS